COURAGE T

a collection
of the
writings of Ruth Fawell

with an introduction
and edited by
Alison Leonard Sharman

QUAKER HOME SERVICE
LONDON

First published November 1987
Reprinted June 1989
by Quaker Home Service
Friends House, Euston Road, London NW1 2BJ

ISBN 0 85245 203 9

Cover design by Anne Gregson

Printed in Great Britain in Palatino 11/12
by Headley Brothers Ltd, Invicta Press,
Ashford, Kent and London

Contents

Introduction

People making their first acquaintance with the Religious Society of Friends often ask: 'But what is it—with no priests, creeds or set words of worship—what is it that holds you together?' One vital answer is: we are held together by sharing. Week by week in local Meetings, those who gather in worship also gather over coffee, in discussion and study groups, for pot-luck lunches and visits to each others' homes.

Another part of this sharing is done in print. For a Society of fewer than 20,000 members in Great Britain to sustain three regular journals is remarkable, but essential. In these journals Friends do their weekly, monthly and quarterly sharing of deepest experiences, of doubts and finding, of researches and reviews.

There are a number of Friends who are regular contributors to these journals. They take the risk (for risk it is) of offering to a wider public their flashes of inspiration or gropings towards insight. Their writings provide a real source of nourishment to Friends and other readers of Quaker literature.

There are a few contributors whose writings are of such consistent quality and inspiration that there is a clear need for it to be made available in more permanent form. Such a writer is Ruth Fawell. I am one of

1

very many who could mention, off the top of my head, a dozen articles by Ruth over the years that have inspired and challenged me, and that is without taking into account her two deeply moving and honest pamphlets, *Death is a Horizon* and *The Relevance of Courage*, both of which are now out of print. So the Literature Committee of Quaker Home Service decided that a collection of Ruth's writings should be published, and I leapt at the chance of editing them.

Ruth was born in 1898. She lost her mother when she was 12, and this traumatic event gave her a profound awareness of the effects of loss and grief. She worked first as a nursery teacher in London's East End, and then trained as a social worker. It was during her period of training that she met and joined Quakers. There followed a busy time of work, marriage and parenthood—and a separation from her children necessitated by the war, when she returned to full-time social work as an organiser of Citizens' Advice Bureaux. After her children's return from evacuation she became involved in the post-war upsurge of work for children and young people in the Society of Friends. In 1946 she wrote *What it Means to be a Quaker* (revised 1957 and 1963) followed in 1952 by *Worship and Our Quaker Meeting*. Her husband died suddenly in the year she became sixty. She originally wrote *The Relevance of Courage* in 1965 as a series of talks given in the BBC's Overseas Service, and its publication was followed in 1970 by *Death is a Horizon*. In 1965 she visited her daughter and family in New Zealand, travelled widely among Friends and returned to live there for several years as extended

2

family and part of the New Zealand family of Friends. She returned to Britain in 1980, and now lives in one of the Quaker sheltered flatlets in Winscombe, near Bristol.

Ruth often refers to the *Advices and Queries*. The Advices and Queries are part of the central literature of the Religious Society of Friends. Contained in a small booklet and revised in every generation, they are guidance and inspiration and challenge. They are also to be found in *Church Government*, the second volume of the 'Book of Discipline', the principal Quaker book of British Friends. The first volume *Christian Faith and Practice in the Experience of the Society of Friends* comprises in anthology form the accumulated experience of Friends, both individually and corporately.

In these pages will be found some famous Quakers: George Fox, who between imprisonments rode and strode the country in the seventeenth century proclaiming the gospel of 'that of God' in everyone; William Penn, the founder of Pennsylvania; as well as modern Friends like the American Rufus Jones and the British broadcaster Gerald Priestland. Ruth sometimes refers to 'ministry', which among Friends most commonly means 'spoken contributions in meeting for worship'; to the annual Swarthmore Lecture which is given at the time of Yearly Meeting; and to the Quaker journals, the weekly *Friend*, *Quaker Monthly*, and *Friends Quarterly*.

We have called this collection *Courage to Grow* because the themes are spiritual growth through everyday experience and the courage which this requires. Courage could be defined as bravery by those to whom bravery does not come easily. Ruth has found, and describes for us so clearly that we can use her experience to enlighten our own, that it is not only the huge moments of life that need large doses of courage. The small trials, too, day by day, require courage if we are to use them to grow in love rather than to retreat into self-absorption or 'why me?' Joys as well as disasters need this spirit, to save us from smugness and isolation. Above all, perhaps, the note that is struck throughout her writings is one of en-couragement—a celebration of the friendship and trust that we can all offer each other, so that each is enabled to go forward in their life rather than back.

ALISON LEONARD SHARMAN

PART ONE

Worship

1
Findings

Your speech is simple, my Master, but not theirs
  who talk of you.
I understand the voice of your stars and the silence
  of your trees.
I know that my heart would open like a flower;
That my life has filled itself at a hidden fountain.[1]

It is more than forty years now that I came in contact
with Friends—a wanderer as I was from the Anglican
fold and a seeker among many denominations and
faiths. I met Friends as a group of workers and students when I was studying for my Social Diploma in
Bristol. I was drawn to them as people; I liked their
concern for others, their respect for them, their freedom and tolerance and openness, their directness and
integrity and 'baked-throughness' and the natural
way they could talk about religion. It became clear to
me that they had found some source upon which to
draw for strength that was not known to me, and I
asked two of them to take me with them to their
meeting for worship. This they somewhat
unwillingly did.

How well I remember the setting and the silence—
that wonderful welcoming silence, filled with a sense
of praise and glory and awe in the presence of a power
beyond my own small self and the worshippers
gathered so quietly there. Of the ministry of the spoken word I recall nothing, though nothing jarred or

spoilt the homecoming after many wanderings. The treasure I had found seemed startlingly simple and I held this treasure quietly to myself, exploring its significance, feeling it almost too good to be true. Part of its simplicity was that I and others were to start just where we were at that moment and proceed at our own pace from there. How blessed that there were no outward restraints of belief. The promptings of love and truth were the starting places, and we could move at our own pace to recognise them as the leadings of God—the beyond which drew me and others on from our limitations and despairs and smallnesses. In hearing the 'voice of this calling', we would come to know also 'the drawing of this love', and so learn a new trustfulness.

Christian discipleship, the way of Christ, replaced theorising about his nature. This did not make things easier, but more real and more demanding, for this way had implications for our daily personal life, our work, for the social order and the international order. The implications however were not being worked out alone, but in a sympathetic community, who believed that everyone has the seed of the divine within them, and who looked for and found in the meeting for worship the source of living power and the light which shone out in fresh insights and a sense of 'stayedness'—stability and rootedness—which made for a quiet centre beyond all stresses and strains. Not for cosiness—comfortableness—but a deep and necessary comfort in response to trust.

Wonderful to feel that we are just to start where we are—less wonderful to be left there. Often we Friends do not help others to grow when they come amongst us, and yet the Advices and Queries[2] rightly stress the need for continual growth in mind and spirit. 'Are you striving to develop your mental powers, and to use them to the glory of God?' and 'Do you keep your mind open to new light from whatever quarter it may arise?' ask the Queries. And when I was at the Quaker college, Woodbrooke, one of the features of life there which most impressed the students, many of them not Friends, was the way in which old as well as young Friends not only saw the need to go on learning all their lives, but took continued joy in the adventure of discovery that this learning involved.

It is because the learning process is continued throughout life that Friends are seekers as well as finders—not one or the other, but both. One only has to think of the need for a continual search for fresh language, unsoiled by use, to know that we *must*, if we care about truth, continue to be seekers. We may have a firm hold on old truth ourselves, but unless we are eager to find new ways of expressing it we may be unable to speak the word of life to others just when they most need it.

It would be hard to over-emphasise the importance in the anonymous city life of today, with its increased loneliness, of small centres of love and concern and support in day-to-day living and in the times of crisis in personal life. Friends of mine in other churches have told me that it is this sense of loving community that most impresses them in Friends' practice—something of the caring of the extended family now so often missing in the life of the West—something of the caring at its best of 'the beloved community', a caring which can be both practical and spiritual, a sort of divine common sense.

When I was living for more than two years in one of the North Island cities of New Zealand, I felt it was primarily this sense of deeply based concern which held together our small and not very strong Friend group. It was our needs as well as what we had to give that brought us together, our need for sympathetic and upholding understanding in our community concerns as well as friendliness, respect and appreciation of our value as human beings, and our recognition of shared values beyond the purely material ones. We were drawn into the meeting for worship as to a source of strength and joy and peace, to be raised beyond ourselves in recognition of that which was greater than ourselves and sent out refreshed, steadied, inspired and encouraged. There in New Zealand as here in England we have learned to listen to one another, to respect the sincerity of one another's opinions, and to love and care for one another.

The more experiences we have of really listening to one another, as in the worship-sharing and creative listening of small groups, the more we find unity with one another. It is when we won't listen, won't really attend to what others are saying and bluster on with our own intolerant opinions, that we go so badly astray in our self-righteousness. Friends have been given the key to living and working together as a group—to learning within the group life, 'building one another up and helping one another' as the

Advices put it. It is a most precious gift, so don't let's lose it, as we may be in danger of doing, by default.

2
Hold Fast to Beauty

Recently I was taken back in thought to my childhood and encouraged to pick up the strands of permanent and persistent values which my parents and my early life had given me. It made me realise anew how, side by side with a deep caring for those deprived of good health and housing in the city slums of Manchester, my parents had given me an intense love of the trees and flowers not far from our city home, as well as those farther afield in the then easily-reached countryside. The poetry we read aloud together at home with our parents was another way of learning awareness, and holidays at our grandparents' farm in Lincolnshire, where we ran free in the meadows and woods, confirmed (fortunate children that we were) our looking and our loving. In spacious spring visits we lived out our imaginary life, perched up in the blossoming apple trees, or visiting Legsby woods to gather moss and primroses and violets to decorate the village church for the Easter festival.

Sometimes we became impatient, as children will, when my father insisted on consulting tree and plant books to identify specimens. But along with his thirst for information and his desire to train our powers of observation went the bestowal of what, looking back, seems infinite time to let us become part of the natural world and love it. So that, even in my saddest moments since those early days, I have never felt alienated from that world of plants as I have, at times, from the complex world of people. In grief, a rose beside my bed, seen when I awoke, would say to me more vividly than words that the divine reality was still there. 'He rests and is not gone'.[3]

Something of this came back to me in one of our recent meetings for worship when the phrase 'hold fast to beauty' was spoken in a quite different context. It was a word of life for me—a liberating word. There is so much in the *Advices and Queries* and in the Book of Christian Discipline about our relationship with one another and our responsibility towards the world in which we live that I have longed at times to cry out, 'Stop! It's all too complicated. Just look and love and realise that the Word has been spoken, with no words said!'

Perhaps even the liberating words 'hold fast to beauty' are too strenuous a way of putting it, and 'let beauty hold you' needs to be said. 'The beautiful', said Hegel, 'is the spiritual making itself known sensuously. It represents, then, a direct message to us from the heart of Reality; ministers to us of more abundant life.'[4] I am quite sure there are times when God says to me, 'Relax. Open yourself to the greenness of the grass, to the colour and patterning of this particular snowdrop. Just look and love.' At this moment the poet can help us more than the moralist, since the poet's eye is fastened more intently upon the small wonders through which the large significances

12

shine. Don't point the moral, just let the small wonders speak for themselves.

We have some wise and eminently sensible words in our Advices which direct us to 'cherish the beauty and variety of God's world', to 'remember the value of beauty in all its forms', and to realise that 'God's good gifts are for all to enjoy'[5] and that we should learn to use them wisely. I have a feeling that the poets and artists get nearer the heart of the matter for me, and that only poetic language and the stroke of pencil or brush can approach the piercing quality of ecstasy which the colour and shape and patterning of ferns and foxgloves can arouse in my consciousness.

Turning to the New Testament, I am glad that Jesus had something very relevant to say about the enchanting world of flowers. 'Consider the lilies of the field, how they grow. They toil not, neither do they spin, but even Solomon in all his glory was not arrayed as one of these.'[6] To 'consider' seems to imply looking and loving, and also a treasuring and cherishing of the divine life embodied there.

Our Quaker poet, Clive Sansom, spoke of one way of liberation from our human complexities—a very direct way, beyond moralisings:

Do not observe, become,
become the flower rejoicing in the achievement of
    its mission, the insect
ascending the slope of leaf. Climb with the bee
over the flower-sill into the scented cave.
Do not observe, become. For as our love goes out
and our imagination transforms us

13

into the thing we love, we share creation,
see as the spirit sees.[7]

There are important moral issues on which we
know that we are called upon to take our stand, so
why is 'moralising'—an insistence on pointing out
the moral implications in a situation which should be
allowed to speak for itself—now 'out' for me? Why, I
ask myself, were so many of the Victorians and
Edwardians eager to point out the moral, and why did
I as a child of my time positively lap up that attitude?
Perhaps one of the valuable lessons that life has
taught me is that while holding firmly to the law of
love as I read it, I am to resist pointing out the moral as
I, limited being that I am, see it. I think that Zen
Buddhism has much to teach us here about just looking and loving and letting 'beyondness' shine
through, without feeling the urge to explain and
justify.

Contemplation is an end in itself, as well as one of
the chief ways of praying. It is a wordless attention to
an experienced part of the goodness and beauty of life
which opens out into a deep thankfulness and joy. So I
want a poet, Gerald Bullett, to have the last word:

Be still, my soul, consider
the flowers and the stars.
Among these sleeping fragrances
sleep now in your cares.
That which the universe
lacks room to enclose
lives in the folded petals
of this dark rose.[8]

14

3
Joyriding on an Escalator

There is something quite special about relationship with one's grandchildren, perhaps most of all in earlier childhood, when one slips into the garden of Eden with them for a spell. I don't even want to analyse what is so happy-making about this two-way relationship, although I constantly dwell upon it as one of the remarkable bonus joys of these later years of life. It is an experience that I have tasted for more than twenty years now, with six very different variations on the same theme.

Recently I had my eleven-year-old granddaughter from the farm staying with me for a few days in Auckland, the largest and also the most sprawling city in New Zealand. There is much here for a country child to enjoy—beautiful beaches on the harbour mouth, with swims and picnics, museums, trips to the islands and to extinct volcanoes, the zoo, town shopping and art galleries and libraries. What would she most enjoy, ready to enjoy everything as she is by nature, and now at the stage of partly child and almost young adolescent? The peak point proved to be riding up and down on the escalator in our new downtown shopping complex. It was a sort of secret pleasure, for she would quietly disappear and later return with eyes shining after yet another joyride.

Since she was here a month ago I have often smiled to myself as I decide to go joyriding too: soaring up on

15

joyful happenings and perceptions, and riding down carrying them to meet the next bit of everyday life.

Two years ago, during one of those stormy grey patches that we all live through, I wrote in my daybook: 'I'm wanting to keep a few pages of this book for thankful joys'. I headed the pages with the words of Beaumont and Fletcher, 'Oh, let my joys have some abiding!'[9] I left five pages free, so that I could write down those joys just as they came to me, especially on dark days—but five pages was not enough, not nearly enough.

I wonder what your joyriding entries would be. Here are some of mine, more or less taken at random:

a) Skies, golden pink at sunset, barred with indigo or melting into a clear shell pink, fleecy white clouds floating on blue, green light near the horizon. The wide expanse of sky from my window.

b) Real friends—K,D,S,M,J and others—in the family as well as beyond it, whom I can trust and love and talk to freely, knowing that they are open to understanding and will throw my dross away.

c) Watering the garden in the cool of the evening, hearing the splash of the life-giving water and feeling its power to sustain and renew life after the heat of the day—the scent of sweet peas, roses and honeysuckle.

d) The dear fun with children—laughing with them, picture-making, reading stories and poetry, printing leaves, sharing their fresh enjoyment.

e) Thinking of the noble companions ahead of me on the road—Edwin Muir, Robert Frost, Van Gogh, Dag Hammarskjöld, Arnold Toynbee, Teilhard de Char-

16

din—those who help me each day to go on making my daily discovery.

f) The purity of the Garden of Eden in Mozart's Flute and Harp Concerto; the inexhaustible depths of Beethoven's last quartets.

g) The good smell of baking bread. Producing a well-cooked simple meal.

h) Sleep, that wonderful liberation from the sometimes too heavy burden of consciousness.

j) The tremendous variety of colours in their stirring beauty—my glowing embroidery silks and wools, the scarlet of poppies on my wall-hanging taken up by the redness of the books and candles.

k) The 'cantus firmus' of the embrace in which I am held if I will let myself be held by its sound—the return home, when home is badly needed, to the One in whom I am always at home if I will let myself come home.

The pages of 'abiding joys' are full in my journal and I have set several pages aside in my new daybook for future delights, for, as Tagore says, 'Wherever there is a bit of colour, a note of song, a grace of form, there comes a call for our love.'[10]

4
Little Bird and Holy Dove

Some time ago I took part in a meeting for worship at which personal life experience seemed to me to be used in ministry in a not very helpful way. This led me to feel that I needed to do some hard thinking about the right use of such experience in ministry, especially as I myself have over the years shared with Friends some of the deeper experiences of my life in a different medium, writing. I have learned that honest sharing can help others. At the same time I have felt the vulnerability of such sharing.

Christian Faith and Practice in the Experience of the Society of Friends starts with a chapter containing the spiritual experiences of Friends from the time of George Fox down to those of the present century. I am thinking, in what I am saying now, of personal experiences that cannot, in themselves, be regarded as 'spiritual'—just everyday happenings, some very ordinary, others at a deeper level, as well as the more searching and testing experiences of loss, bereavement, broken relationships, severe illness, failure and death.

First of all I would like to offer you some reflections on everyday experiences being shared in our meeting for worship. You may recall Gerard Hoffnung's cartoon of a dear little old lady with a parrot perched on her shoulder, giving ministry of 'the little bird said to me on the way to meeting' variety. The little bird's chirpings cannot be quite the end of the matter as far as ministry is concerned, since all spoken ministry, however simple, should come from the promptings of the Spirit and in some way contribute to the deepening of the sense of wonder, awe and awareness of transcendence of the worshippers.

In my local meeting we often have with us a good

number of children, as well as young people in their teens. Friends naturally feel concerned that spoken ministry should speak 'to their condition' as well as to that of older Friends. On one occasion we were offered stories of birds, cats and sheep observed by the speakers, but somehow on that occasion something essential to spiritually nourishing ministry seemed to be missing. We all failed there, because if the speakers did not bring out this element in what they gave us, we other Friends had the task of doing so. Here are some words from George Gorman's Swarthmore Lecture, *The Amazing Fact of Quaker Worship*, which are apposite:

> What we say should always have the innate capacity to transcend human experience, although remaining part of it, but nevertheless should point to an enlarged dimension and vision of life.[11]

The task is not only laid upon the speaker, but also upon us, the fellow worshippers, of sensitively drawing out the 'enlarged dimension' from preceding ministry, if this is needed. This is something very different from pointing the moral of a story! How grateful we feel to those Friends who have the ability to do just that—help us to move towards an 'enlarged dimension'.

Although our bird/cat/sheep meeting seemed to me to have been unable to achieve that enlargement, we have had other very telling meetings for worship which have started from small everyday experiences. One such that I recall began by a Friend telling us about the rubber bands, dropped by our local postman, which she found and picked up as she went along the roads of our village. (I too regard these rubber bands as treasure trove.) She spoke of our need to extend our own enclosing bands through reaching out to others and to the world around us. The simple opening moved into a particularly fruitful meeting in which the hidden divine life was revealed. On another occasion the collecting of discarded buttons, called for in a Blue Peter television programme and spoken of while the children were still with us, led us into the recognition of the meaningfulness of small and seemingly insignificant contributions to the building up of the Kingdom of Heaven, and we moved together into the 'enlarged dimension'.

This bringing of all experience 'into the Life' seems to me to apply equally to the sharing of deeper life experiences in spoken ministry. The inward question *has* to be answered: Is this experience to be shared in meeting or is it for me alone? This must be answered before one rises to one's feet. In general such experience as has been digested and worked through emotionally seems to have a better chance of helping others than words spoken while the speaker is still out in the stormy sea, unable to keep his or her head above water; though, as I write this, I can think of immediate exceptions—meetings for worship which have been called on to do loving work on spontaneous cries from the heart. It helps the worshippers if such calls are free from egocentricity, if they are not just using the meeting as an outlet for emotional release, if they avoid triviality and are as brief and honest as possible—and have within them the seeds of transcendence.

As there is an undoubted need in present-day life for people in trouble to find helpful ways for emotional release, I am sure that we Friends need to see whether such outlets as creative listening groups, 'days of communication', and the clearness committees which have been found so helpful overseas, may not help us too, new as they still are to many of us. Some of our large city Meetings are, I know, aware of how such methods can be rightly used and are already using them to advantage, especially among younger people.

In whatever way we bring our personal life experience into our meetings for worship, our task is that of following 'the natural, though extremely demanding, path of seeking depth through ordinary everyday living and seeing such experience as that which can be interpreted in terms of transcendence',[12] bringing it, in George Fox's words, 'into the Life'.

5
Joy in the Silence

It had been for me a joyful meeting, with the Easter Day realisation of the 'ocean of light and love' flowing over the 'ocean of darkness and death',[13] and of the true resurrection, the sprouting of the seed from the seemingly dark ground. A realisation, too, of the unconditional way of living which we are asked to accept in the New Testament story of Jesus' life on earth, where dark as well as light was woven into the pattern of the whole.

But near the end of this same meeting, one Friend had spoken sadly of the lack of relevance for him of Jesus' sufferings because he himself had never experienced anything of that painful story of betrayal, denial or crucifixion in his own personal life. This brought a vigorous older Friend to her feet after meeting had ended, to ask whether we do not dwell too much on suffering. She did not find our pensive faces very joyful! 'Tell me,' she said, 'how do we experience joy in our silence together? *Can* we experience it, without song, dance, children playing and laughing, outward celebration?'

Undoubtedly we do need times together for joy to be expressed in song and dance, in drama and painting and poetry—times too when we can just make a 'joyful noise unto the Lord' together. But my answer to her question about joy in the silence is still 'Yes, a thousand times yes! And when we do this, the joy percolates through unmistakably into the ministry, and flows back again into the stillness'. The Light Within is not just something thought about, though we do need times to think about it too, times of learning. The Light Within is something experienced and felt right through one's being, and this feeling has something of the nature of keeping 'a-top' the world, in George Fox's telling phrase. When he met an obstacle he tried to get 'a-top of it', and in that clearer air we can breathe freely and joy may flow into our lungs.

Sometimes, when we feel submerged by the

harsher experiences of life, we bear a heavy burden into meeting with us, and put it down and are aware of a power beyond our own, helping us to come 'a-top the cumber'. I have been impressed in rereading the gospel of Mark, to find how unconditionally Jesus lived in a world which, though different in many ways from our own, was still an amalgam of good and bad. Fox, in speaking of the uplifting power of the Inner Light, called it the 'topstone'. I see it as a cairn at the top of some beloved hill, where we stand open to the wind and the sky and breathe freely.

Is it a rare thing to experience this joy of being 'a-top' the world when we sit together in our meetings for worship? I certainly experienced it the very first time I was taken to a meeting nearly fifty years ago in Bristol. I can think, too, of a number of different settings in which it has again come through quite unmistakably for me, and I will try to describe briefly three of these.

I don't often remember the spoken ministry, though when I do it can indeed become part of my life. But I do remember well the feeling of many meetings for worship I have attended, including one where I understood no word of the spoken ministry, when a group of us stood at worship under the pine trees, beside a lake, one very early morning in Japan, and knew deep within us that we were there in the presence of God and of one another, happy in our unity.

The first of the three meetings for worship I want to describe is a meeting with a great many young parents with small children and babies. The room is full as we begin to centre down to a background music of babbling. There is no sense of strain, of anxious parents keeping their children in check: every now and then a questioning toddler sets out on a journey across the room. The stillness grows deeper. Presently a Friend is on her feet speaking to us of the following day as one designated by the United Nations as the international day for the elimination of racial discrimination. It is fitting that we should remember those who are victims of racial prejudice and injustice, both in our own country and overseas—those who have been broken in body or spirit, and those, too, who keep alive the structures of prejudice. As we unite in this ministry a very small person climbs down from the bench where he is sitting with his parents, crosses the room, seats himself on the hassock of an older Friend, takes from her with a smile her key ring held out to him and offers her a little hairbrush. While we listen, the Friend beside me is gently brushing the restless toddler's hair. He settles down contentedly until the children leave us. The room is filled with acceptance, tenderness and concern, and the message emerges from dark places into a thanksgiving for the richness and variety of life—an accepting joy.

My second meeting took place on the Sunday of a working party's visit to a meeting house of Wanganui Friends in New Zealand. For ten days about forty Friends had been living together at the new Friends settlement just coming into being. Again the room was crammed to the doors with young and old, many of them people who had been working together, playing together and being quiet and listening to one another during the previous week. We had for that short spell become partners in the new venture; we had, too, been much tendered by the severe handicap of Philip Smithells, one of the original settlers, who was actually in the last week of his life when we left to return home. We entered into the commitment of those Friends who were the first settlers and a great feeling of the triumphant quality of the divine at work in ordinary human beings swept through us, so that in a short hour twelve brief messages of faith and commitment came through. That might have seemed questionable in the everyday setting of our home meetings, but here it expressed our togetherness and 'the divine impulse given and received'. Another 'joy experience', where the silence in which those two- or three-minute utterances were held played as essential a part as the speech, since it was the soil into which the seeds were dropped, and from which, in the rich humus, the plants grew.

Finally, joy in a Friends meeting for worship held in thanksgiving for the grace of God in the life of an old and loved Friend who had been a source of strength and love in her family and in her local country community and of faithful commitment among Friends. Funeral services in crematoriums are not necessarily seen as occasions of joy, but there, through the quiet and helpful introduction to Friends' way of worship given for the many people present who were unused to it, a ministry of thankfulness grew. At one point a group from another church sang a hymn, and words were spoken about our Friend's caring and enduring life. The beautiful words of William Penn, 'The truest end of life, is to know the Life that never ends',[14] were read. As for the silence, it glowed with rejoicing thankfulness.

So *can* we experience joy in the silence?

6
Worship and the Shining Conker

Yesterday's meeting for worship was the meeting for worship of the shining conker. It started with the account of how a small boy on a walk with a group of unknown other children, feeling rather lonely and isolated, came upon a chestnut tree, and discovered the joy of finding the lovely shining object that emerged from the rough ugly outer shell—its shape, its smoothness to the touch, its rich colour, and its wonderful shining quality. The contrast was a moment of revelation to him—'like people', he commented. A moment of revelation, momentary as it may well be, is a moment of joy and awareness ready to become a song of praise and thanksgiving. It is in itself a song.

Very recently our media of communication have been filled with horrifying scenes of violence—racial tension in our own country and terrorism further afield. It is against a very dark background that I want to dwell on the bright flowers of joy and praise. In our world creation and destruction go side by side, and the darker the darkness, the more we need praise and thanksgiving. This is not to pretend the darkness is not there, but it is a necessary proclamation of the truth we believe, that the 'ocean of light and love flows over the ocean of darkness and death',[15] and that the kingdom of heaven for which we are working *is* a kingdom of love and beauty and truth that calls for our awareness, recognition and commitment.

The poet Rilke has a poem starting with the line: 'Oh poet, tell us what you do?' and the poet's answer is 'I praise'. The poem goes on to ask: 'But those dark, deadly, devastating ways, How do you bear them, suffer them?'—'Because I praise'.[16]

Rilke is telling us in this poem that we can only meet the devastating happenings in our personal and our community lives from a background of light, and acknowledgement of all that is good, all that unlocks the doors of the prison of self. We can't help people caught in the hell of 'resentful living' because of injustice and hardship, by living ourselves less than thankfully. 'Resentful living,' says Neville Ward, 'is the alternative to thankful living. It is the condition of being against God and against life, unable to love either, and this is precisely the Christian idea of hell.'[17]

At a recent study weekend, a Friend expressed the pain he experienced at being the 'thankful privileged person' he felt himself to be, rejoicing in the abundance of God's goodness to him in a world where so many are in trouble through natural disasters as well as through the injustices, cruelties and ordinary human frailties of their fellow men and of themselves. It is a tension we have to learn to live with, and I find Rilke's thought that we can best live it through praise a fundamental one.

Praising God does not mean flattery or adulation on our part. Praising is lifting up, extolling, all the goodness and beauty and truth that we know.

The psalmists were well aware of this and I am glad the Psalms were part of my early Anglican upbringing. The psalmists burst out with songs of exaltation for all the goodness of the good: 'I will be glad and exult in thee', 'I will give thanks to the Lord with my whole heart', 'Oh come, let us sing unto the Lord: let us heartily rejoice in the strength of our salvation', 'Shout to the Lord with loud songs of joy'. And all this joyful praise goes on in the Psalms side by side with the singers' honest expression of sadness and at times despair over the savagery of the human heart.

In the Anglican communion service come the words: 'Lift up your hearts!' spoken by the priest, followed by the response, 'We lift them up unto the Lord'. How much we need this exhortation if we are not to get bogged down in the darkness of despair! Our meetings for worship are an opportunity for us together to do this lifting up, and daily too we have this need to lift up our hearts to all the beauty and truth and goodness that we know. We neglect to do this at our peril. The sculptor Barbara Hepworth said, 'Nowadays there is nothing done which conveys the féeling of praise. We have no time for praise. And yet, without this feeling of inner wealth that can afford to praise we are injuring ourselves and each other.'[18]

However far at times I may get away from holding fast to praise, I do feel deeply convinced with Rilke that praise is the clue to true living and that it is closely linked with trust, and when I get away from this deep conviction, I ask to be brought back to it again.

Rilke's poem goes on to speak of other situations in which we need to praise:

> And then the Nameless, beyond guess or gaze,
> how can you call it, conjure it?—I praise.
> And whence your right in every kind of maze,
> in every mask, to remain true?—I praise.
> And that the mildest and the wildest ways
> know you like star and storm?—Because I praise.[19]

We best know the shining beauty of our chestnut by praising.

7
What! No Flowers!

One of the loveliest gifts in the dark time of February is to be given (or to find) some of the very first flowers that appear. Besides daffodil buds from the Isles of Scilly, my January birthday brought me a little bowl of moss, and resting in it primroses, golden witchhazel and three snowdrops from a local garden—the snow-drops pure white with their 'triplet of green-pencilled snow'. I have no language to express the sense of wonder that flowers arouse in me, nor how they speak to my condition.

All through the year at our meeting for worship, on the table, we enjoy the varying flower arrangements which a different Friend makes for our delight each

Sunday, flowers from Friends' gardens as well as leaves and ferns lovingly picked in nearby fields. They brighten the rather dark and vast room in which we meet—a room that also serves as a school hall.

Imagine one Sunday in the autumn when the table was bare of anything but the Books of Discipline and Bibles. Picture, too, the first ministry of that day being on the speaker's disappointment at missing the flowers in our midst, and his realisation of how we so often take their colour and beauty for granted and only realise it when it is not there. Picture, too, the shock I felt when I then looked up for the first time to the table, to realise that *I* was the person who should have brought the flowers on that particular Sunday. As I sat there I could see in my mind's eye those golden chrysanthemums and the tawny brown and orange beech leaves and seed heads and grasses that I had picked along the old railway line the previous day, had arranged in a blue and gold Breton jug, and put carefully outside my flat in the open air to keep the flowers fresh. How could I have forgotten them at the last minute before setting out to meeting? But there it was—in spite of my own passionate love of flowers, I could, and had!

The spoken ministry wove itself around our perception of the bare table—our expectations, the many other gifts that people bring us, some hardly perceived, others taken for granted and only noticed when they are missing, our need to respond to that call of Jesus to really *see* and *hear* and *understand*, our humbling dependence on other people for the things that we enjoy every day. Towards the end of the meeting I felt compelled to admit that I was the person who had forgotten to bring the flowers, and that I needed Friends' forgiveness for my forgetfulness. Out of a rather bleak situation, a really good meeting for worship had developed.

Some years ago in the Philadelphia *Friends Journal* there was an article by Joe Havens called 'Disappointment, a Chariot of Truth'. I had been impressed by this at the time and cut it out to keep and ponder upon, and I found it when I came back from meeting. I am sure the writer would have said that at that meeting we had been riding the chariot of disappointment. He said in his article that we Quakers expect a lot of life and that our faith in the Inner Light in everyone leads us to expect a high level of behaviour in our families, our friends, our meetings, and ourselves. I know this in myself and I know too how easily and sharply I do suffer a sense of disappointment, not least in myself. We can't help being disappointed, we can't always help causing disappointment; and if we are made that way, we shall experience disappointment sharply, so first of all we have to recognise honestly that we are indeed disappointed.

Now, what are we going to do with that feeling? Joe Havens tells us in his article that the early Buddhists rested their whole religious practice on 'the assumption that life was essentially and inevitably disappointing, and that only through recognising the bald fact and looking into its origins could peace be attained.' The sources of disappointment lie in our own natures and in our ego-drives—for comfort or recognition or security or certainty of faith. Seeing clearly the root of our disappointments will help us take the next step and learn to let go of many of our wants.

It is natural that I should *want* things to go my way, should *want* harmony and happiness in my surroundings. But I need to see the world as it is in itself, not just as I would wish it to be. I must move towards what Joe Havens called 'radical unprogrammedness' and so open myself up quietly, beyond my disappointment, to what that particular moment is saying to me, to 'new light from whatever quarter it may arise'.[20] If only I will recognise, and then still, the strong claims of my ego, there are divine leadings which I shall see, and hear, and feel.

PART TWO

The Spiritual Journey

8
Negative Capability

I am challenged in the depth of my life by such demands as George Fox's 'Walk cheerfully over the world answering that of God in every one'[21] and that of Paul in his letter to the Philippians, 'You are to shine like stars in a dark world and proffer the word of life'.[22] Many years ago I met a prayer which I still pray fervently, 'Let not my gloom darken the light by which others have to live'. My conscious mind holds firmly to the faith that 'the ocean of light and love flows over the ocean of darkness and death' and that thereby I may know 'the infinite love of God'.[23]

And yet that bright star-like life to which I aspire is constantly threatened by the darknesses of Auschwitz and Hiroshima, as well as by all the negativities and blacknesses that are poured out by the media in constant profusion, and by the losses, hardships and sadnesses of everyday life. The 'word of life' which we all long for must include darkness as well as light, but in such a manner, if we can discover it, as not to 'darken the light by which others have to live'. That we can only do when we have come to terms with the darknesses within us and outside us. So the challenge is to discover how to deal with the negatives without pushing them out of sight or being overcome by them.

The phrase 'negative capability' met my eye in an article about John Keats' Letters. The poet was using it in a rather different, but related, sense. 'Negative

35

capability,' he wrote, 'is when a man is capable of being in uncertainties, mysteries, doubts, without any irritable reaching after fact and reason'[24]—the basis of imaginative activity whereby a poet can accept both woes and delights as experiences. I shall be using the phrase to mean an ability to make the best use of all experience, dark as well as light, that comes our way. I believe that when we in our lives work to bring good out of evil, we are working with the grain of the wood instead of against it, with the on-going purposes of God instead of against them, and that we shall be given strength and help as we do so.

I want to speak briefly of ways of coming to terms with my own darknesses that I have found helpful. Some of them may be pointers for others, whilst for some of naturally cheerful and positive temperaments, I may not be speaking at all to their condition. I am not dealing here with depression as a pathological condition, where special help is needed, but with a depression which many of us experience in varying degrees at times and which forms a temptation to despair. It can be understood as having its roots in heredity, in environmental factors in early childhood, and can be precipitated by situational problems which none of us can avoid facing. We shall not become people who 'make the best use of everything' without finding out for ourselves a true discipline accepted from within—the sort of discipline we all need in learning an art.

One of the most important realisations of Quaker faith when I first came among Friends in my twenties was the emphasis I found there that worship and work, spirituality and action were firmly wedded to one another. The whole tenor of the Advices and Queries is that all life is one. Drawing strength from beyond ourselves, we are to be what Dietrich Bonhoeffer called 'the man for others'—the person for others which Jesus was. Our relation to the beyond-ness that is God and to our neighbour is stressed without perhaps showing how each person must first come to terms with his or her own pain, loss and hardship before he or she can truly help others to come to terms with theirs. Perhaps some of the 'fresh light' which we are advised to be ready for at all times 'from whatever quarter it may come'[25] is the psycho-logical knowledge that has come through to us especi-ally through Jung and others whom we are to 'approach with discernment'.

My reading has shown me that that negative think-ing causes depression and pessimism, that we our-selves are responsible for it, and that we can learn to turn every negative thought into its positive before it goes down for filing in our subconscious. I may, for example, experience a difficult and disturbed person contributing unhelpfully in meeting. I can let this spoil my whole experience of meeting or see it as a minor set-back which must not be allowed to spoil the whole and I can put it in its very minor place. We have many small negative experiences which we may meet destructively or constructively. This sounds simple, but can be quite an exacting exercise.

We all know that a trusted friend with whom to share and get rid of our negatives is a treasure—and should be a two-way one. Failing this, a journal or an odd bit of paper to rid oneself of negatives can be helpful, as also the habit of talking aloud to oneself in an empty room ('Just how childish can one be!'), or to God—mostly what have been called 'arrow prayers' ('I do need you', 'Be there at my waking this new day'). I have always been greatly helped by the Advices and Queries on the God-ward and other-person sides of life, so that many of the suggestions that follow link closely with insights gained through Quaker teaching. Here are random ideas which I have found useful to ponder on:

Look at the positive things in your life and talk positively to yourself.

Understand your feelings. But focus on behaviour and action.

Seek help when you need it and recognise your own dependency needs. Don't always insist on being a helper; let yourself be helped, or, as the Advices put it, 'Be ready to give help, and to accept it'.

Use 'words of life' (I keep my own anthology of these to which I return in times of need).

Pray. The Advices say 'Make a quiet place wherein you may learn more of the meaning of prayer and the gladness of communion with God our Father. Encourage in your family life the habit of dependence upon God's guidance and on his help for each day's need'.

38

Don't be too hard on yourself and then you won't be too hard on others.

Banish false expectations of others and of yourself; make only realistic demands on others.

Focus on a right assertiveness; express in love and in a tactful way what you feel. Is this the Quaker as well as Paul's emphasis on 'speaking truth in love'?

Be careful with introspection; limit the time you give to it.

Learn to cope with pain, going with it rather than fighting it or allowing yourself to be submerged by it.

Choose healthy, undramatic ways of dealing with hardship, loss, pain and extra strain of all kinds.

Accept the tension between hope and despair and so learn to live with your tensions.

Learn to laugh—laughter is relaxing and helps to preserve a true sense of proportion. The Advices on marriage remind us to value a sense of humour.

Accept responsibility for the depression you feel; recognise, if need be, that it is more or less with you from time to time, that you have dealt with it in the past and that you will do so again.

Make play part of your life and regard it as important, not just a frill, but one of the 'signals of transcendence'.

Try to find a healthy routine that brings real satisfaction to you.

Give thanks with all your heart for the beauty and goodness you encounter in life.

Finally, we are asked to let go, to relax and let the spirit descend upon us and guide us into the truth of the situation in which we find ourselves.

Life is a tremendous learning process and we may find to our astonishment that our failures and errors have been more creative than our successes, leading us to deeper understanding of ourselves and of others, and to new growth and a sense of blessing. In Hebrews, we read that Christ, the light of the world, still had to learn through the things that he suffered. There was no pretence that the darkness was not there.

We find ourselves in the area of paradox as we set out to learn negative capability. Developing psychological insights can help us supplement and ground more securely our other-directedness, for we shall never love God and others aright unless we rightly value ourselves. We are called to be aware that God uses darkness as well as light to effect his divine will and that while we learn to endure and use the darkness, we can still appeal to the same God as our steadfast source of strength and learn to 'sunbathe' in his light and love.

9
Have We a Secret Discipline?

The learning process that we undergo in the physical life is often paralleled by learning on the spiritual side of our lives. Years before anyone talked about psycho-somatic medicine, I came in my medical social work to what, fifty years ago, seemed the startling realisation that mind, body and spirit were wedded to one another. Although many doctors in their wisdom recognised the need to treat the 'whole' person, the now fully accepted ideas in this field seemed strange and, to many people, unacceptable.

People seem to shudder nowadays at the mention of the word 'discipline', and a friend of mine, seeing the title of the Book of Discipline, told me that she found the use of the word very off-putting. Perhaps this word (like the words 'love' and 'God') has been used so loosely and sometimes so threateningly that we need to translate it mentally before we can have the benefit of its real meaning in our daily lives. Two dictionary definitions are 'training by exercise' and 'bringing to a state of order and obedience by training and control'.

Both are relevant to Bonhoeffer's concept of 'a secret discipline'. He speaks of this more than once in his *Letters and Papers from Prison*. 'What is the place of worship and prayer', he asks, as he explores a new way of expressing faith, 'in an entire absence of religion? Does the secret discipline at this point acquire fresh importance?' And again, 'A secret discipline must be re-established whereby the mysteries of the Christian faith are preserved from profanation'.[26] So this 'training by exercise' is to be pursued in a hidden and not a boastful manner. The idea reminds one of the words of Jesus about praying 'in secret'.

This 'training by exercise' reminds me of the

experience of learning to write in script. It looked so beautifully easy and attractive but the training by a series of strenuous exercises set by the art teacher was quite another matter, and at the end of the first term one could understand his glee in being able to eliminate anyone who could not accept the discipline of learning a new skill. I only just survived.

Another lesson in accepting discipline in a quite different field came my way after a domestic accident, in which I fell off a table on to a tiled floor and broke my ankle in such a way that it could not be put together again. After the ankle joint had been done away with and the ankle had been turned to solid bone, a long grind under the skilled guidance of a physiotherapist followed for me. She and the orthopaedic surgeon certainly both disciplined me hard in order to make me completely mobile again. The goal of complete mobility was an important one for me and my family, and this was triumphantly achieved. I was advised to keep up certain exercises involving both my legs, and this I did for a time, until I wearied of them. Trouble with the extra strain on my uninjured foot began to develop, and the warning came from a chiropodist this time. 'Soon you will not be walking at all!' he said. It was then that I accepted once and for all the at times tedious discipline of daily exercise that preservation of mobility involved. Did I sufficiently desire to be self-motivated and to be 'serviceable' for my family and friends and neighbours, to persist in my mobility training? The answer was clear: 'Yes!' I would still wake up in the morning not feeling at all like giving the ten minutes involved, but every failure to keep up the self-imposed discipline would have to be compensated for.

I know by experience that the same rule holds for me in the realm of the spirit. I know only too well that I shall only remain mobile, as well as at times even just manage to stand my ground, if I hold firmly to my own hidden spiritual discipline as I have been clearly shown that I have to maintain my physical one. The relevance of the former will be shown as clearly as the latter—how I deal with the adversity that inevitably comes to everyone at times, whether I am able to live from the quiet centre through thick and thin, whether I am able to practise the goodwill, the love shown so clearly in the life of the one I follow, whether I can accept forgiveness when I fail, as I often do, and whether I can begin afresh and grant to others fresh beginnings too.

I am helped in my discipline by the Quaker Advices and Queries, to which I often return as though to get my bearings again when I have lost my way. There I meet the reflective wisdom of our Quaker group as it has been gathered together over the past 300 years. I use the New Testament and the Psalms in somewhat the same way—not reading daily passages, though sometimes undertaking regular study, but turning to these well-tried sources to check the route. Righteous indignation or unhelpful gossip make me turn to the New Testament for light on the way that Jesus dealt with such situations, or to such an Epistle as that of James. All this, and the use of many and varied sources (not necessarily Christian) come into my early morning time of reflection, which is a vital exercise for me. I also use it to get rid of some of my sadder or badder thoughts, so that I do not need to let them loose on someone else's day. There, waiting on God, I sort out my priorities.

Because I come of a family which has a dark thread of indigo (the colour of depression) running through its pattern, I start my day by doing some relaxing exercises—letting go the tension in each part of my body, becoming at ease, quiet and open. These I follow by a positive act of trust such as 'Lift up your heart; I lift it up unto the Lord', or 'Know that you are in the hands of the Lord and that whether you live or die you are the Lord's'. This is followed by a brief act of thankfulness, before I go on to hold up those in need, those whom I shall meet that day, those who are far away. If I am very tired I have words at hand to help me through these acts of opening, receiving, carrying living water for others. Words of Dag Hammarskjöld in *Markings* are of special help to me there, because maybe he too knew only too well those threads of indigo. And so he can help me to set out on my journey with: 'Thine the day, Lord, and I the day's'.[27]

10
'Speaking of God to Man in Dreams'

It was not until I read Howard Brinton's *Quaker Journals*[28] that I was struck by what George Fox says about dreams. He speaks about varieties of dreams— some caused by 'multitude of business', others he terms 'whisperings of Satan to man in the night season', and yet others as 'speakings of God to man in dreams'—a truly lovely phrase. For this last kind of dream ample precedence, he says, is found in the Bible.

The 'speakings of God to man in dreams' have to be subject to what Howard Brinton calls the 'divinely illuminated conscious reason' so that each dream, into whatever category it may fall, comes under the scrutiny of the light. At its best, the Quaker faith has kept a balance between inward vision and outward evidence, and it is this disciplined but also relaxed walking of the tightrope between the two that has made for what may be called the Quaker characteristic—at its best—of divine common-sense. Inwardness must never be wholly detached from outward checks, based on 'divinely illuminated conscious reason' both in oneself and others.

I have been a dreamer all my life as far back as I can remember. In earlier days it was a family joke against me that all my dreams were sad or bad. I don't remember in earlier life finding those dreams so meaningful as many later dreams seem to have become, for often hard and painful truths have come to me in later life through dreams. I seem to pour out into them my feelings about grief and loss and the inhumanity of man to man (rather in the same manner as animosity was poured out into a 'Hate Journal' in that extraordinarily helpful book, *The Amazing Fact of Quaker Worship*[29]) instead of letting my despair loose upon other people in everyday life. I would not call them 'whisperings of Satan to man in the night season' but, in so far as negative despairing dark thoughts present one with a temptation, they do fall into George Fox's 'whisperings' of darkness. They are usually of a very personal nature, giving me something to think about, put right, a challenge to which to respond, but like very personal messages that form in one's mind in a meeting for worship, they seem to give a word spoken to myself alone, or only to be shared with a trusted friend or with a small intimate group such as a worship sharing group.

However, once and memorably, I had three dreams within one week of each other, which could clearly and unmistakably be called 'speakings of God to man in dreams'. Many years after the time of acute grief in my personal life that brought them forth, they seem to me to be dreams that can well be shared with a wider group, for they were indeed words 'of hope and faith and pity and love', given when most needed, received thankfully with both hands. They left me feeling that I had discovered the whole secret of being, the key to all life. Deeply meaningful, deeply religious, they yet never mentioned the name of God, or Christ.

Because I wanted to treasure them, I wrote them down before the end of the week, partly so that I would not change them or colour them more vividly in retrospect. Here in their simplicity they are, written down more than fifteen years ago:

The First Dream

I was at a Quaker summer school in a lovely part of the countryside. The school was well-organised and there was a big crowd of friendly happy people of all ages, extremely talkative. The talks and group discussions were held out of doors under beautiful trees. There were rambles during the afternoons during which people talked and laughed a lot.

I was so lonely there that I walked away on my own. I tramped a long way until I was weary and I found myself in a doctor's waiting room in London. As usual it was very full, although the room was much larger than usual—almost a hall. As the patients had to wait so long, the doctor had arranged that small plays should be acted to entertain them. These were at the end of the room behind an improvised curtain. I stood near the door alone.

The curtain was drawn back and a simple nativity play with gipsies in it began to be played. I was surprised and delighted to find that some of my closest friends were taking part in the play. As I stood there someone came up behind me and put an arm about my shoulders, so that I was no longer alone. I felt deeply comforted.

47

The Second Dream

I was being swept along in a broad swirling river towards the open sea. It was a wild stormy day with dark rain clouds racing along overhead. The reeds and the trees on the river banks were being tossed wildly in the wind which blew over the face of the waters. I was being rushed along at the swiftest part of the current. I could not direct my course, nor could I strike out for the banks, though now and then I tried to take a stroke or two to keep to something that might approach shaping a course. It seemed as though I must perish in such turbulence.

Then, as I was being swept along, I heard a quiet voice say, 'Take hold of the rope'. Beside me in the water I saw the end of a very strong rope. 'Hold it firmly, but easily,' said the voice. I took hold of it in the way I had been told and imperceptibly the waters became calm, or I became quiet in their midst. I looked again at the rope and saw that it was not just an end. It stretched behind me as well as in front, and I knew that I only needed to hold it like this to be taken down to the sea. I knew, too, that it had been there all the time. I was no longer afraid, and the waters that had before seemed hostile, sweeping me down to the sea against my will, now seemed friendly.

I awoke from this dream feeling that I had discovered the key to all life. The dream had such reality for me that I had to touch a rope similar to the one in the dream that I saw in a shop some days later, and in bed I felt compelled to lie in the position I had taken up in the dream as I lay in the water holding the rope.

48

It was days before this first vivid feeling of discovery and reality left me.

The Third Dream

I came down in the morning and went to the front door, as I usually did to see whether the front step needed washing; birds often built their nests on the ledge above it and there were constant droppings on the step. Through the glass top of the door I could see grey fog blotting out the oak trees across the road, and even the rose bushes in the front garden with their last November buds. It was not a tempting world to look out upon—bleak and wintry and dark—but I opened the door.

And there, to my complete amazement, lay on the front steps, covering their entire length, the most beautiful bouquet of garden flowers that I had ever seen. At the heart of it were the deepest of velvety roses—the flowers I most love—and around them were delicate ferns, cream, pink and flame roses, and every variety of michaelmas daisy from deep purple and blue to the tiniest of fairy-like white clusters. A profound joy and thankfulness filled my being, and I bent down and picked up the flowers and carried them into the house.

This third dream, like the second one, had such an extraordinary vividness that I was impelled to go downstairs and open the door in the way I had done in the dream, and look at the doorstep where the flowers had been lying. Again the dream was more real than reality.

The test of the truth of these dreams was not just

what happened in the following weeks—how I lived them through in that crisis time into life, with inward vision and outward expression welded firmly together—but how they continue to speak to me, especially in other dark and stormy parts of the journey, of the divine beauty given and received, the voice that speaks to man in time of need, the human divine companionship.

11
What Did My Accident Mean?

In a recent 'Thought for the Day' radio talk the speaker said, 'I've come to God through happenings, people and things'. This is true of me too.

One happening that brought God very near to me was the time when I fell off a kitchen table and broke my ankle so badly that the joint had to be done away with. During the weeks of hospital treatment that followed, I and my family were showered with love and support by a very caring meeting. In the middle of my long hospitalisation Joan Mary Fry, a member of my Meeting and a Quaker 'guru' if ever there was one, visited me and asked me the question which startled me then, 'Do you know why you have had this accident? And why just now?' It was a pertinent question to ask.

Recently I caused another type of accident. It did not lead to physical damage to myself or others, but could well have done so. The resultant damage to property was not great but, as all accidents do, it caused disturbance and quite a lot of trouble and work to a large number of people. Again I received no reproaches, only kindness and reassurance. Someone said gently, 'I hope you're not worrying about this accident.' What was going on inside me was much more like a painful, humbling search, and a voice I recognised saying to me in a very insistent way, 'What is *this* accident saying to you? I ask you to give an honest answer within yourself and not avoid the issue.' I was aware of God as a voice seeking for 'truth in the inward parts'.

My answer, of course, will be a very personal one in terms of the sort of person I am, with my own particular defects and imperfections, so the answer my insistent inward voice drives me on to find cannot be another person's answer. I would like, however, to share with you some reflections that have come to me since this last accident.

I have recently been reading Winifred Rushforth's *Something is Happening*.[30] She wrote it when she was 96 years of age, and put into it for the lay reader the results of her work as a psychiatrist and her conviction of the interdependence of body and spirit. She does not speak of accidents, but there is much to be learned from her chapter entitled 'My Illness'. She asks what is the inner psychic element lying behind the outward bodily happening, and points out that the individual's illness is a mode of communication, a way of the unconscious aspect of our life talking to us and asking us to listen and to understand. She suggests three ways in which our illness may be speaking to us; I will pick out one of these as being possibly relevant to the accident situation: 'It may be confronting us with the fact that our life is too full, we are too busy, we have "no time" for what needs to be done. Our illness forces us to take time to *be*, not only to *do*.'

An illness, says Winifred Rushforth, may have positive value and out of it further understanding of life may emerge; the important task is to understand the motivation and to ask, *why* am I ill, and *why* just at this time? This runs parallel with those questions asked me years ago by Joan Mary Fry about my accident. Even a minor fall in old age may speak of an unrecognised diminution of bodily control which the person finds unwelcome, yet needs to become aware of for their own safety and that of others.

Some accidents, as I well know, are due to carelessness of one sort or another, and I know that each of these two accidents of mine, apart from other elements, undoubtedly contains a certain degree of carelessness. Von Hügel said, 'Caring is the most important thing: caring matters most'.[31] He was speaking there, I imagine, about care for other people. Caring in the sense he used it means a true carefulness—for others, for oneself, for material possessions, for our environment, for the one world in which we live. At one end of the spectrum stands the fussy person, who exaggerates carefulness until it becomes a pain in the neck, and so confuses true priorities; at the other extreme is the careless person, who does not show proper respect for material possessions, for other people, for his or her own welfare. My own hatred of fussiness shows me where my own failings undoubtedly lie! Both my fussy friend and my careless self need to discover where true carefulness lies and to correct our own imbalance. Carelessness can never be regarded as relatively unimportant.

We have to be aware of our humbling interdependence, and increasingly learn that we are beings of one vast interrelated world. We cannot just say that we are so small and insignificant in face of the whole that it does not matter what we do. The longer I live, the more convinced I am that we are infinitely responsible for our own infinitesimal piece of reality.

Today we are suffering badly in a truly painful way in our community life from lack of carefulness—care. The individual cannot opt out, but has to throw his or her own weight wholeheartedly on the side of caring. Walter de la Mare, a poet very dear to me, spoke of true care in his poem 'Winged Chariot':

> The true, the guileless, meaningful and fair
> Rest for their essence on our heed and care;
> These are Earth's everything, Heaven's every-
> where,
> However small the commons we ourselves may
> share.[32]

12
'Use Words as Though God-Wrought'

I ask myself why it is that I feel so strongly as I do about the subject of gossip. Is it that I myself am liable to fall into what my dictionary calls 'idle or loose talk'? Is it because other people I know well have suffered from what Query 13[33] speaks of as 'unkind gossip', which is there partnered with 'hurtful criticism'? Is it because I see it as a threat of a very serious nature to community life, concerned as I have recently been in the life of an intentional community? Why do I want to thump my objection out, when chatting about people and their varied lives can be so fascinating, and when this talk contributes so much to the spice of life?

I think it's because I am painfully aware of how such talk can degenerate by almost imperceptible degrees into something which lacks true charity and respect for others, the discretion which we would wish to have shown to our own affairs, and which the people talked about would certainly not enjoy if they could hear it. Country people and especially women, as I know from my experience of overseas countryside life as well as in this country, are particularly prone to it, and those brave spirits who attempt to live in community are not immune. I know well that it is the impulsive rather than the cautious personality who can so easily step over the fine line between enjoyable chat into the indiscreet talk which is tinged with judgmental attitudes, and from real fun into naughty fun.

When I was a schoolgirl with a quick and sometimes mocking tongue, I remember my wise and loving father (who never overdid the 'moral social talks' as my own daughters have called parental homilies) warning me seriously against making disparaging

54

remarks about other people, whatever the grounds of my belief. Later, in my early twenties, he wrote me this advice again in a letter, which points to the fact that I must have needed the earlier advice.

In Auckland Meeting there was a Friend who would say of someone, 'He (or she) is a really *pure* person.' When I questioned her about this, she explained to me that she meant the person never said a harsh or unkind thing about anybody and was a person of complete integrity. A community is indeed fortunate when it is made up of such 'pure' people. It is a *sine qua non* for keeping the water of community life clear and sweet and unpolluted. In what I am saying here, I am by no means ruling out serious consideration of character 'in the round', warts and all, which is essential to fuller understanding of others as well as helping self-understanding.

From my own reflections on a subject like this, I find it helpful to turn to the New Testament to see what it has to say, as well as to Friend sources. The Epistle of James[34] gives a very down-to-earth picture of living out the Christ life in everyday life, and here are some relevant thoughts and directions James gives us: 'A man may think he is religious, but if he has no control over his tongue, he is deceiving himself; that man's religion is futile;' 'The tongue is a small member, but it can make a huge claim—the tongue is in effect a fire;' and 'Brothers, you must never disparage one another. Who are you to judge your neighbours?' I have heard people speak of James' letter as 'unspiritual', but to me its quality of bread baked right through speaks strongly of the 'purity' of which our Auckland Friend was speaking.

Some fifty or sixty years ago, our Friend Henry Hodgkin made some 'suggestions concerning our attitudes towards those who differ from us', and his suggestions speak to my condition. Here are one or two which seem to me to be particularly important: 'I always seek to discover the best and strongest points in my brother's position . . . I will try to avoid classifying him . . . When others criticise I will try to bring out favourable points . . . If I have been betrayed into criticising another, I will seek out the first opportunity of finding out if my criticism is just . . . I will not listen to gossip or second-hand information.'[35]

A footnote here, though: if you refuse to listen to gossip as Henry Hodgkin recommends, beware just how you do this. I remember a young daughter putting me right years ago because I did the right thing in the wrong way in such a context. 'You sounded dreadfully priggish in the way you did it!' Our *hows* are as important as *what* we do, and it is often through the *hows* that we show our real consideration for the other person.

There is a beautiful poem by Richard Church about our use of words, and it ends on the note of 'purity' of speech:

Here then is need for caution. Be admonished
To use these daily words as though God-wrought,
Magical master-keys to light and glory.[36]

13
A Further Forgiveness

I thought that I had taken in and could go along with, even though I did not always succeed in practising it, the Gospel teaching on forgiveness. But in the past two years I have found that my understanding of forgiveness just does not stretch far enough or deep enough, and that I have had to do some more searching.

The main theme of the story of the Prodigal Son is fully acceptable to me. When the son 'came to his senses', as the New English Bible says, he decided to go back to his father and say that he was sorry and he was able to say, 'Father, I have sinned against God and against you; I am no longer fit to be called your son.' His father, who had seen him while he was still a long way off, and whose heart went out to him, ran to meet him, flung his arms round him and kissed him; the son stammered out his repentance, and was fully and rejoicingly forgiven.

How wonderful and liberating such forgiveness is. We can identify with both the father of the story and with the son. We have all experienced the giving and receiving of this sort of forgiveness—'the answer to the child's dream of a miracle', as Dag Hammarskjöld called it, 'by which what is broken is made whole again, what is soiled is made clean'.[37] A trail of unhappy consequences may still lie in wait for the repentant one, but the liberating moment of the son falling into the open arms of the father has taken place for both—a tremendous moment of awareness and healing love that will carry both forward over the stony path of mending what is broken and washing what is soiled.

I remember years ago kneeling by a small daughter's bed and trying to help her to feel sorry for her part in an unhappy rift that had taken place between her and her father—just to feel responsible for her side of what had gone wrong, instead of dwelling, as she was doing, on how he had offended. Finally she went to him and whispered in an almost inaudible voice, 'I'm sorry, Daddy'. I could only see her lips moving and could not hear the actual words. He looked across to me and I nodded 'Yes'. It was a Yes that said that he, another obstinate person, must accept even that inaudible murmur of apology. Afterwards he said to me pretty fiercely, 'Did you expect me to accept that mumble?' and my reply was, 'Yes, I did, knowing how very hard you yourself find it to say that you are sorry.' For the little daughter I was urging a course not just for that moment but for a whole future in which only the liberation of asking for forgiveness and receiving it can keep life sweet and sane—something that Dietrich Bonhoeffer said in his 'Wedding Sermon from a Prison Cell', and which remains with me as a sheer necessity in true family life:

In a word, live together in the forgiveness of your sins, for without it no human fellowship, least of all a marriage can survive. Don't insist on your rights, don't blame each other, don't judge or condemn each other, don't find fault with each other, but

58

accept each other as you are, and *forgive each other every day from the bottom of your hearts.*[38] (My italics)

If another person comes to me and says sorry for what he or she has said or done, my heart rushes out to meet that person. As the poet Blake has said, mutual forgiveness of each vice opens the gates of paradise.[39]

But what if the other person does not say sorry, just is not sorry? What then? And if you yourself have an impulsive nature that makes you rush into a plea for forgiveness that meets a blank refusal, what then? I can still remember when I was a child—and a passionate child—holding my older sister against a wall and saying, 'I'm going to *make* you forgive me', after a quarrel. She had a cool temperament, and despite my violent pinioning of her, I did not succeed in making her do as I wished. She just said coldly, 'You find it pretty easy to say you're sorry.'

There are the exuberant ones who can easily rush into the father's arms, but I have come to realise that we are not always cast in the role of the father or the younger son in the story. We may find ourselves in the place of the older son looking on at the seemingly easy apology and the seemingly easy spontaneous forgiveness. The younger brother wasn't saying he was sorry to *him* for wasting the family money, nor for leaving him to do an extra share of the work. The elder brother reacted badly, with resentment. What was really being asked of *him*? He wasn't in the centre of that lovely warm scene of forgiveness which I understand so well; he was left on the sidelines with the offence—

the irresponsibility of his brother with all the consequences that came in its train, the pain that had
been inflicted on his father by the repudiation of the
younger son when he claimed his inheritance and
went away, the probable hostility to his hard-working
older brother. Looking at the older brother intently,
we can see ourselves and our difficulty of winning
through to the forgiveness beyond forgiveness, the
forgiveness of Jesus' words on the cross, 'Father, forgive them, for they know not what they do.' Perhaps
one can better grasp something of that further forgiveness of another person if one sees it as compassion for erring humanity, for faulty persons like
ourselves, which has to grow side by side with con-
demnation of the cruel and the irresponsible and the
self-righteous deed or word.

'Forgiveness', says Dag Hammarskjöld, who had to
live out this further forgiveness,

> breaks the chain of causality, because he who for-
> gives you—out of love—takes upon himself the
> consequences of what you have done. Forgiveness
> always entails a sacrifice.
>
> The price you must pay for your own liberation
> through another's sacrifice is that you in turn must
> be willing to liberate in the same way, irrespective
> of the consequences to yourself.[40]

It is still a mystery to me—this forgiveness beyond
forgiveness—but it is a compass in my hand pointing
clearly the way I must travel, turning my gaze from
that compelling person who lived that sort of forgiveness out in his daily life back on to those with whom I

am in daily contact, as well as upon my own heart
with its stupidities and sins.

14
Changing the Lights

Every now and then a phrase or line of poetry or a
verse from the Bible begins to haunt me. As a dream
does, that phrase may voice a question, or bring me a
vital message, or even offer me comfort when comfort
is needed. Such a phrase has been with me recently. It
was part of a quotation from George Eliot's *Middlemarch*, which was sent me on a greeting card. This is
the passage from which it comes and the emphasis is
mine:

> The presence of a noble nature, generous in its
> wishes, ardent in its charity, *changes the lights for
> us;* we begin to see things again their larger, quieter
> masses, and to believe that we too can be seen in
> and judged in the wholeness of our character.[41]

George Eliot would certainly not have been
visualising this in terms of traffic lights, but that was
the first picture that came into my mind. There are
times in our lives when the lights seem to persist in
registering red, and we can be held up for what feels
to us a very long time. We seem to be 'stuck' in our
relationships, our work, or in our spiritual life—dry
times that have to be endured. Will the lights never
change and give us the signal to move ahead? And

then in great matters or in small, the green light appears and we are liberated. Or, perhaps closer to George Eliot's thought, we find ourselves living day by day in a grey, sunless world, although we know that the sun is shining elsewhere, and suddenly, or perhaps imperceptibly, a ray of gold breaks through and we find ourselves in a world of light again.

This can come about through our encounter with a 'noble nature' such as George Eliot speaks about, and I am conscious that in early life I met a number of 'changers of the light' for me, both in everyday life and in books. Most of us have had heroes and heroines, and as I remember it, that was what took me into London's East End in my early twenties, after I had read Margaret Macmillan's vision of a garden nursery in a Deptford slum.

The changing of the lights may happen, as in early life, in highly coloured and dramatic ways, but recently I have been aware of this coming about in very small ways indeed, and not always through other people, but through nature—the sight of a delicately patterned snowdrop in very early spring, the glory of the evening sky—as well as through art in its varied forms.

As life goes on, we discover that we are called to live with uncertainties and darknesses and yet to live with hope and to hold fast to the certainties that we *have* found. I think it was Leslie Weatherhead who said in later life, 'I believe more and more in less and less,' and I am with him on that. One of my unshakeable certainties is that we are called by that insistent inner voice, which I know I neglect at my peril, to remain open to and aware of the light we are constantly being given. More than once Jesus said to his disciples, 'Can't you see, can't you hear, can't you understand?' For he was, indeed, a changer of the lights for others. They only began to see what he was really saying after his death. We are as responsible as they were for opening ourselves to the elusive movements of the spirit in our lives, and we know that we can be as stupidly unaware as they often showed themselves to be.

The 'changing of the lights' for me is something that I pray not to miss. It can take place through just a smile, a touch of the hand with real caring, the discovery of a new writer who speaks to me, the gaiety of a Vivaldi record, a visit, especially from someone younger than myself, a fresh perceptive message in meeting for worship, a good laugh with a friend restoring balance in life, someone giving me a breath of the hills or the sea, a piece of encouragement in my own sphere of action or expression, a tree in winter, a poem—there is no end to the changing of the lights for me. I have a book where I put down some of these 'light changing' experiences, which can also be called blessings or acts of grace. I can then reread them in grey moments to remind me of the tremendous outpouring of love in my life.

Eckhart said, 'What a man takes in in contemplation, he must pour out as love.' My thankfulness for the changing of the lights that I have received cannot just end with me. It asks to flow out to others, and to be open to the opportunities that come my way to change the lights for others.

PART THREE

Old Age, Death and Grieving

15
The Later Years

What should the years in the third period of life mean, the years from the age of sixty or sixty-five onwards? Are they to be regarded as merely negative, as they tend to be in present-day society, or should they be positive and meaningful and bring their own satisfaction?

In the early years of retirement there is clearly an opportunity for new adventure, and many are able to grasp it. These people are often those who are already rich in resources of all kinds and who, before the sixties come upon them, have been able to cultivate friendships and develop new skills and appreciations which can come into their own in retirement. Happiness in retirement and successful adjustment are based on having a sense of purpose in life that is not completely dependent on our work but on the development of creative interests and friendships throughout our lives—not expecting to develop these suddenly at the moment of retirement—and on feeling valued and needed and respected as persons, not just as workers.

Here speak two friends of mine about the joys of their retirement, the one retired for twelve years and the other much more recently. One speaks of the satisfaction of the voluntary work in which she got involved and adds:

In addition to these commitments I have had a great

deal of joy and happiness. There is the ease of visiting art galleries and museums and of getting to know the highways and byways of one's own city . . . Reading has been a great enjoyment . . . and I have also been able to attend a study group.

Sometimes I try to discover what it is that has so specially appealed to me in retirement, and the main thing, I am sure, is the sense of freedom that one enjoys—freedom to choose activities, to enjoy sunshine and rain, to have the pleasure of entertaining one's friends and even of making new friends . . . I have a deep feeling of gratitude for the kind of 'irresponsibility' which is surely permissible in old age.

Another Friend, who speaks of how tired she was towards the end of her professional career, says:

I think the thing I value most of all is that I can now be *available* to my friends and others in all sorts of ways. I find it wonderful to have whole days and weeks in which I can choose among many delightful things what to do. I have always enjoyed my home and now it is my pleasure to keep it neat and clean and welcoming, a place where I can cosset friends if they need it. I enjoy working in the garden, too, in spite of rheumaticky bones. I like to go visiting: I am rich in loving friends and relatives, nieces and nephews, all of whom are glad to see me. Included in my wide circle is, of course, our Meeting. What an enrichment of life it has been to belong to a community of like-minded Friends, to have worshipped with them, to have shared their joys and sorrows—the successes, the failures and mistakes that make up the life of the Meeting—and to have been able to serve in many ways.

She speaks of turning outwards, away from 'my little self, my lord', and names among these the joys of bird watching and language study, and finally quotes Tagore's poem, 'Because I love this life, I know I shall love death as well', adding: 'Because I loved my work, I knew that I should love retirement as well'.

All retired people are not as fortunate as these two friends—not as rich in friends and relations, not as rich in spiritual and mental resources nor as adequately provided for financially. We need to think of these others, and how best we can help them. Loss of money earnings cannot be minimised, for even if many of us have adequate pension schemes and so lead a free and happy life ourselves in retirement, we know that many others live near the poverty line and that others lead lives that are to some extent restricted in freedom of movement and choice of activity by slender means. Other serious problems that are encountered in later life are loss of purpose, loss of status in society and loss of companionship, which can lead to such strong feelings of bewilderment and apathy and despair that illness and early death may result. Any one of these causes or a combination of them may lead to suicide. The feeling of unwanted-ness in an active, working society can be one of the worst problems of all. Perhaps one of the greatest needs of today, side by side with schemes to prepare people for retirement and provide centres for companionship and visiting schemes for the house-bound, is to show the real respect and love for older people which gives them a place in society that satis-fies their need to be needed.

Sooner or later the urge to outward activity dies down. Are we still needed then? 'Old men ought to be explorers', says T. S. Eliot.[42] What is to be their explo-ration when their energies diminish and ambitions proper to earlier life lie behind them?

If we live long enough, the time will come when we are asked to listen and encourage, to stand back and let others go forward. 'Try throughout life', say the Advices, 'to discern the right moment to relinquish responsibilities which should pass to those younger than yourselves'.[43] This is a hard lesson for many of us to learn, but with what gratitude we look back to those fine disciplined spirits that taught us this lesson through their own lives. There is something pathetic about the older person who clings to office when there are younger people ready to assume it.

The adventure of life does not cease as we grow older, but it may be difficult for us to discover another rhythm after our busy, over-active working lives. Gradually we are being led in the direction of being rather than doing: it is a process which has been developing in all those moments of choice that have called for renunciation from particular things, for detachment from time and place and for acceptance of our incomplete and limited human condition. It is a great joy in later life to be more readily available to one's friends; to be able to be completely 'there' for others is such a great need in the world today, and for lack of it many suffer from loneliness. Younger friends of mine have told me, too, that other qualities of life for which they specially look to their older friends are stability and firmness of faith, wisdom and serenity that is not placidity and self-satisfaction but a 'calm brightness'—all gifts that may flower specially at this later season, as well as the gifts of reflection and prayer for others. The answer to the geriatric social worker who, in telling me of her problems, said longingly, 'Shouldn't our Christian faith give a triumphant quality to old age?' is most assuredly 'Yes!'

16
Borrowed Time

I am wanting to say something about the 'borrowed time' as it has been called of very old age—over 75 or so. I do not want to minimise all that makes this period, which I did not ask to enter with its diminishments and losses, possibly the most challenging stage of my whole life. And yet . . .

The Challenge of a Long Life is the title of a book by Lily Pincus, written in her early eighties and published just after her death at 83. Her background was Jewish, her faith of a triumphant quality. Her book points up so well what I want to say, for it emphasises (without minimising the negative aspects) the element of challenge in this often unwanted situation. Our Advices too bring out the challenge: 'Each stage of our lives offers its own fresh opportunities. Face with courage the approach of old age, both for yourself and for those dear to you, realising that it may bring wisdom, serenity and detachment'.[44]

I find that what Lily Pincus has to say about the fundamental importance in the development of our personality from birth to death of learning to cope with loss and separation, is really vital. Our acceptance of the crises of loss throughout life without self-pity will help us to respond in the same way to the inevitable and increasing losses of old age: loss of physical powers, hearing, sight, energy, mobility—as well as losses sustained in our emotional life, the loss of close family and friends. Side by side with the acceptance of loss situations, she speaks very perceptively about accepting the negatives of life. 'Now, in my old age', she says, 'I realise how important it was for my development to experience and accept at an early age the negative aspects of the place and the relatives I loved *and to go on loving them*'.[45] The emphasis is mine, for this is a hard lesson for me as for many others and I am still being called to learn it. One of the insights of Friends that I have always treasured is that learning is to continue throughout life, and this learning is to be not only on a mental but also on an emotional and spiritual level.

Lily Pincus was a social worker with skills in the counselling field, and she stresses the continued need to make and maintain significant personal relationships in old age, since *the ability to relate is the key to life and growth*. As I write, I am thinking of a dear old friend who remained in her own home with family

72

support until she reached the age of 89 and then had a severe hip accident and died soon after the operation. She was able to keep her independent life with help, to be in close contact with family and friends and to pour out love and welcome and cheerfulness to all who knew her. No egotism got between her and 'answering that of God in everyone'. Not all old people are endowed with such gifts of character or are so favourably placed. Peter Townsend in his studies of old age[46] stressed that old people in general long to have their families—people they love and relate to—within reach of them. If circumstances take one out of easy reach of loved family and close friends in old age, we must not be surprised if an emotional crisis has to be faced. Just as the muscles and intellect can be harder to exercise in old age, so it may be harder to form emotional relationships. I found this a disturbing fact to take in when I came back to this country after living for the greater part of twenty years overseas. Truth *is* disturbing, and if we remain open to it with God's help, we must be prepared to be disturbed.

Triumphant facing of loss and negatives is not the only feature of later life, vital though it is. The dear 89-year-old Friend of whom I spoke was endowed with a zest that kept her eyes bright and sparkling, coupled with a vivid interest in all the everyday things going on around her. Sheer enjoyment of beauty and of play come in here, as does the delight of grandchildren and maybe great-grandchildren and contacts with the young in the community around us. All this is part of 'living until we say goodbye'.

One big realisation in later life for me is how thankful I am for the difficult and painful experiences that I have lived through. I know that they have come my way because I am being asked for growth in awareness. There is a lot to be learned about the bearing of pain, both physical and emotional, including the increasing tiredness and the unpartnered loneliness of extreme old age.

Finally, I am conscious at this stage of life of our need to grow in awareness of the world within, beyond that natural longing of ours for touch, sight and sound. Only so can we really 'carry our dead with us' quietly and thankfully, and be free for the task of the Advices—by our thought and prayer 'liberating love and power in others'. I have been given good models among Friends, of old people who have shown us what a unique opportunity old age can give for the fruition of selflessness and wisdom and 'of the dearest freshness of deep down things'.

17
'Carrying Our Dead With Us'

A friend's loss of his wife recently has reminded me of one of the memorable experiences of the fifteen or so years I spent in New Zealand. It was the first visit I had paid to a Maori 'marae' or gathering place in Auckland, with a party of 'pakehas'—people of European stock. We were visiting the people of the land, settled there before the Europeans came, a people with a great feeling for their land and for their ancestors.

I had been in touch with the elders of the 'marae' beforehand so that when our party arrived, some twenty strong, we received the customary Maori greeting as we advanced across the grass towards the meeting house. We were told through an interpreter that, in the haunting plaintive 'mihi' (greeting) they chanted, they spoke of bringing their dead with them, and saluted in us the dead we carried with us.

In our party we had with us a member who had recently lost a much-loved adult son; we were aware of her grief and shared it, and I felt pained lest this greeting might reactivate her grief. I need not have feared, for she told me afterwards that she found the Maori message deeply comforting, as she went forward with tears in her eyes. She needed that open recognition of the precious burden she was carrying.

When one of their number dies, the Maori people are well aware of the need to pour out grief, and to share the outpouring with the bereaved person before the healing process of recovery can take place and the move forward to everyday life begin again. Rooted in the soil, and with their sense of the reality of the unseen world, they remind us of that reality and those roots in a way that is badly needed in our modern materialistic world.

Looking back to my own childhood and at my visits to much-loved farming grandparents, I remember feeling something of what my grandmother carried behind the comforting exterior that I knew. I had been told of many of her children dying in infancy, as so

75

often happened in those days. I had been shown their graves in the Lincolnshire country churchyard and so, as I sat cosily by her listening to the moral children's tales she loved, I felt something of what she carried. I experienced it not morbidly, but as a sad-happy thought that brought an awareness of an unseen world, so real to her and only just sensed by the child who sat by her.

The dead may first be carried sadly, as our friend carried her son on the 'marae', or carried joyfully, as did my old friend who had lost his wife after physical frailty and suffering, so that her death was a release and a blessing.

Eric Holttum speaks of Gerald Priestland's insistence in his Swarthmore Lecture that Jesus 'still is', and went on to say,

> But unless you believe that death is a total extinction of every personality, the spirits of all departed people 'still are' with us. My belief is that each has contributed something to the sum total of spirituality 'in which we live and move and have our being'. Departed spirits are no longer limited by physical bodies and are surely integrated with each other in ways we cannot comprehend.[47]

I cannot fully go along with Eric Holttum in his way of expressing himself in such a definite statement on 'departed spirits', but I am with him in recognising that past, present and future dwell in us all, and that the past, into which the person dear to us has in one sense withdrawn, may come to life through us in a new way, and that we are called to open ourselves for their contribution to come through. I wish that I could say that the unseen world in which I believe is always as real to me as the seen and touched world, but it is not so, and I can only pray, 'Lord, I believe that nothing is lost. Help thou my unbelief'.

There is a poem of Anne Ridler's which expresses well this theme of 'nothing is lost' for me. She writes of the death of her beloved father, of the birth of her baby son and all from the past that is bestowed on him. She speaks of the interdependence with the dead as well as with the living. Here is the beginning of her poem:

> Nothing is lost.
> We are too sad to know that or too blind:
> Only in visited moments do we understand;
> It is not that the dead return—
> They are about us always, though unguessed.

As we grow older, I am sure that we are called to hold as firmly to our 'visited moments' as we can and to witness to them to others. We will let the poem's end have the last word:

> Thus what we see or know
> is only a tiny portion, at the best,
> of the life in which we share: an iceberg's crest
> our sunlit present, our partial sense,
> with deep, supporting multitudes below.[48]

18
Coming Through the Tunnel

A friend was telling me about her mother's difficulties in getting going again after she had broken her hip. She said, 'I'm sure that my mother has the feeling of having lost her identity. She has always seen herself as a bright, brisk, sociable little lady in these later years (she is on the far side of eighty-five) and she can't find *herself* in her present slowed-up guise, limping about and unable to go out of doors without help'.

Later in our conversation we were talking about the loss of our husbands—hers two years ago, mine twenty years past. Again she used this phrase, 'I had the feeling of losing my real identity, and I still haven't fully regained it'. I too remembered feeling, all those years ago, 'I don't want to be this different widow-person. I only want to be the loved wife of my husband, no-one else'.

By the time we are very old—over seventy-five or eighty—we shall certainly have faced, and helped others to face, many of these loss situations. For some, perhaps, this sense of lost identity doesn't descend upon them as it descended upon me and my friend. My conversation with her helped me to recognise clearly that I have just been travelling through another loss-of-identity situation, and that I have been finding it painful. Just over a year ago I left the environment in New Zealand where I had been for many years, and where I had a very real place of warmth and understanding and belonging. Our conversation made me realise that I need not be surprised to find that, despite my pleasant situation since my return, I felt a sense of depression and loss. As we advance into our eighties we have to realise, as I and my friend's mother with her hip accident had to realise, that we are less adaptable physically, and psychologically too. Our personal temperament, as well as our limitations in later life, are factors that we need to understand and learn to accept, with the acceptance that we would expect to give to others in a like situation.

In our conversation, we had moved from recognising those loss-of-identity experiences to the realisation of our need to find a new identity—without one's husband, without full mobility, without one's former warmly loving environment. I found myself asking what relation this question of identity has to our faith in the Inner Light, to 'that of God' at work in each of us. For some days I could not see the connection. But my experience is that if I wait quietly and with open eyes, I am given clues which, if followed, lead to new light.

A week ago, during the Field Day of the local wildlife habitat group, we visited a tunnel on a disused railway walk. Tunnels and caves have had a fascination for me since childhood, as they undoubtedly have for many children of all ages. We had been advised to bring torches so that we could observe the tunnel walls with their stalactites and stalagmites. As we entered from a very muddy path, it was a relief to find that the tunnel, so mysterious in prospect, was short (only 180 yards, we were told) and that from the entrance, as one moved into dimness, light showed at the other end—light and grass and trees and sky.

All week the image of the tunnel has been with me, and as the days have passed, the words 'in thy light we shall see light' from Psalm 36 have moved to the forefront of my mind.

Five days after the tunnel walk, I came upon the following passage in a small book called *A Pool of Quiet* by Kitty Grave of the Friends Fellowship of Healing. This particular meditation was based on some words of Rabindranath Tagore: 'Our true life lies at a great depth within us'. Kitty Grave spoke of the feeling we all have at times of being spiritually dried up and of feeling as though our true life were lost. She went on: 'It is perhaps a comfort to realise that this is a common experience amongst those who are seeking the way, and we may forget when these times come to us that there are phases, *tunnels, as it were, through which we must travel. We have come out of previous tunnels and we shall doubtless come out of others, providing we keep our eyes on the gleam of light at the end.* We cannot always tell why these phases come, but let us remember that life is going on—"at a great depth within us". It is not lost'.[49] (The emphasis is mine.)

Our varying loss experiences, dark at the time, seem to me rather like that particular tunnel. Maybe if we were completely faith-filled we would not feel this loss of identity as we travel through our tunnel, but most of us are like myself and my friend, just fallible human beings with temperaments and characters which are not always easy to handle. We have to make our way painfully through, telling ourselves that there is, most assuredly, light at the other end, and that in that light we shall be given more light to find our new identity in the changed situation.

Our teacher on the wildlife walk told us to notice particularly the very rich variety of ferns and mosses on the limestone rock as we emerged from the tunnel into the daylight. Maybe our new identity, when we find it, may include something of that rich variety.

19
How Do We Look at the Fact of Death?

What we actually believe about death and life is perhaps less important than our whole attitude to the fact of death.

Maybe we face the fact of death for the first time when someone near and precious to us dies, and we then wake up to wrestle spiritually with the feelings of anger, dismay and acute deprivation that take us by surprise and question our hard-won faith. Or we may be called upon to stand by another person suffering great grief in bereavement. It is through such experiences that we struggle towards an attitude of our own towards death, so that we can speak from where we stand, and from the acceptance of the strange and paradoxical nature of death, as of life.

Death is part of the story of our life and as natural a

part of it as is our birth. At birth 'the child is, so to speak, thrust violently forth from the confines of its mother's womb, and forced to leave its protecting, accustomed, familiar *milieu*. It is exposed and threatened with complete destruction. At the same time, however, there opens up before the child a wide new world, a new relationship, the world of light and colour, meaning, community and love. Something similar happens to the soul at death. Violently it is taken out of the confines of the body and the world it has known hitherto'.[50]

Death is a necessary part of the rhythm of being, just as sleep is part of the rhythm of night and day, and so is tremendously welcome.

We know the sense of living beyond time and space—in eternity—in the heightened moments in this life, the moments of ecstasy which illumine our everyday world. 'He hath set eternity in man's heart', says Ecclesiastes, and we know this sense of abundant life here and now, an experience not bound up with time and place. Jesus in speaking of eternal life did not confine it to a world outside or after this life. 'Each of us may have a glimpse of it at some point of the intersection of time and timelessness; at moments of great joy or sorrow, at sunrise on a mountain top, at the bedside of a dying friend—moments when we forget ourselves and are lifted up into a higher sphere. Beethoven must have had abundant life when writing the slow movement of his Seventh Symphony, Shakespeare finishing *The Tempest*, Van Gogh painting his sunflowers . . .'[51] Eternal life is not just some future life; it is life in harmony with the true order of

82

things—life lived in loving absorption in what is beyond ourselves, for we are not only material creatures, but have a sense of the beyond that we recognise. If we are to know eternity now and hereafter, we have to nourish this sense of eternal values all our lives by a daily renewed act of thankful love, and a clear obedience to those insights which we are continually being given.

Our mortality gives a circumscribing horizon to our lives and points to our living wholeheartedly today in the light of it, as a poet lives fully in present experience, valuing its precious quality and its poignancy.

If we really live in trust, should there not be a joyful and serene quality in lives approaching the end? How can we be helped to achieve this, so that deep down we have the assurance that 'all things shall be well, and all manner of things shall be well'? This confident trust is not a suddenly developed product of later life as a rule, but part of a long learning process for most of us. It grows through a steady acceptance of change and deprivation throughout life, leading to an acceptance, for those who live on into later life, of what Teilhard de Chardin calls the 'diminishments', the endurances forced on us, of which death is the last to be endured in this life. Another exercise towards growth in trust is through the cultivation of relaxed and thankful attitudes through prayer, and an openness to suffer the many small deaths to self that come to us in our day-to-day life. Thanksgiving strangles self-pity.

Death is a gateway to a new stage of living, approached by many of us with a mingling of fear and of joy, as are all the greatest experiences of life. We cannot and must not minimise the fear that some people feel in facing death and in going alone into the unknown country. There is too the agonising fear of losing those we most love, and the fear of physical or mental incapacity before death overtakes us or those we love. Both these are real and terrible fears. Of the latter, Arnold Toynbee has spoken in his *Experiences*: 'To suffer does not deprive one of one's humanity; senility does deprive one of it, and perhaps the worst malady that can befall a human being is to cease to be *compos mentis* while remaining physically alive'.[52] Yet even when this happens, we can try to dissociate ourselves emotionally from the person who is not as we have known him or her, provide all the loving care that the body and the diminished mental capacity need and tend them as the person we have loved and cared for, knowing that they are already in transition.

Death, like life, is a mystery and when we have said all that we have to say, it still remains a mystery, whether it is a happy release easily achieved or a painful death through physical breakdown, mental derangement or death upon a cross.

20
Facing Terminal Illness

Sooner or later people are brought face to face with those in their terminal illness. What spiritual comfort have we to give to those who know that they are dying and to those who do not know it, but have an expressed or unexpressed fear that it may be so? The question is not only what we say, but what we do and what we are for others. Sometimes nothing needs to be said; the presence of one who cares deeply, and can make the seriously ill person feel this and can help them to rest in the sure knowledge of surrounding love and care, is all that is needed. 'All my loving and caring are for you' can be shown to the ill person, and those who have cared for people in their terminal illness will know the wonderful and strengthening experience of being made a channel for a love much greater and more enduring than one's own to pour through.

This ministry is a very individual and personal matter. Trust in and respect for the essence of the person to whom we speak, sensitivity to their needs, are more vital than any words even when we feel that words are needed. We are asked at times to search for and awaken that of God—the upward-reaching element—in the sufferer's own being and to mobilise a strength beyond their knowing; this applies both to the ill person and to giving comfort to the bereaved. The serenity and love and confidence that all shall be well may be the greatest thing we have to give. We must realise, too, what the dying person gives to us; the dying are already moving into a country unknown to us and may be receiving a sustaining love, a grace and peace and blessedness beyond our knowledge.

To have been allowed to care for a dying person, or just to be there with them, is one of the greatest experiences of life—just humbly and lovingly there, not in any way to interrupt the experience of another person becoming separated from us in spirit and passing through 'the valley of the shadow'. In Walt Whitman's words: 'To die is different from what anyone supposed—and luckier'.[53]

But sometimes there is a longing on the part of the sick person for some 'word of life' to be spoken. It is only by sensitivity that we shall perceive this, since in some instances verbalising can be disastrous. A member of a group with whom I discussed these questions told of an agnostic friend who needed much help in her terminal illness—but silent help. When the hospital chaplain had offered to come and talk to her, she had said, 'Oh good God, no!' but she had a real need for quiet and continued upholding.

For some, this 'word of life' may be an authoritative word that gives peace to that particular person. A difficulty that may arise among Friends is that when people are in a low physical and mental state and their inward authority weak, we have no priest to administer the last sacrament, no compelling outward symbol to speak with power. We must be aware of the need for the spoken word as well as for silent upholding, and must be ready to risk speaking the word of life where it is called for, even though we realise only too well that words can heal or separate. Sometimes we may offer words of comfort that may be pushed away as irrelevant: some of these words may come back later in the quietness. The individual word spoken by one person to another in terms of both personalities can be our strength, but we can fail here at times. The word that we speak must be completely real to us and must come from our own experience.

This 'word of life' may be spoken to someone who shares our faith. How can we help when the other person does not share it? Here the clasp of the hand, the expression of affection and sympathy, the appreciation of the value of the other person may be all we have to give. I remember hearing of a Friend who had visited during his terminal illness an agnostic colleague who had not been told that he was soon to die, of how, when he sensed the need to say something to this colleague, the man brushed aside his words as irrelevant. After this colleague had died, he heard from the man's wife what a depth of sustaining affection from his friends and students had come through in comfort to this man in his last days, a real speaking into the depths of the other. The 'standing by' of another person, whether in terminal illness or in bereavement, is the vital thing—the being willing to be the rock for another. 'Lo, I am with you alway, even unto the end of the world'.

The need for contemporary words and symbols is clear; the call to give a fresh assurance of meaning beyond our outgrown language constantly challenges us. Some symbols, however, have permanent value— the archetypal images of the river, the sea, of light, of the cross, the rose, the garden and the flame.

In many Quaker Meetings it is the practice to ask an ill or old and housebound Friend whether he or she would like a few Friends to join with them in a meeting for worship in his or her own home. When this is readily accepted, it can be an experience of upholding power. The need also has to be borne in mind to visit those in hospital, especially those in chronic illness, and to be sensitive in each individual instance to particular needs. Perhaps Friends differ from other churches in this. Although individual church members or the minister visit their sick and dying members, this corporate worship together might mean much to some.

21
Facing Bereavement

There are losses in our lives of those very dear to us through which we pass serenely, but then there may come the loss of one especially close—husband or wife, child or parent or friend—and our loss seems to be so great, our grief so acute, that we do not know how to bear it. Each must learn how to bear this individually, but it may help us to know that others have been in this dark valley, have not lost their reason (perhaps one of the darkest fears), have learned to endure and to come through to light again. Whether we are among those who know a grief that shakes us so deeply that it seems as though our roots must be torn out of the ground or whether we are among those who are so blessed by temperament and faith that they are carried in quiet confidence through all the experiences of bereavement they are called upon to face, it may still help us to understand the experience of desertion and desolation in the lives of others. It is for this reason that I write of my own experience.

The funeral is over and the strange, unreal days following a death in the family are past. Through these days and through the illness that may have preceded them you, like me, may have felt yourself upheld by a power and a presence that lifted you up and carried you through the first cruelty of shock. During this time I rested quietly in the thought that all was well for the husband I had lost and so all must be well for me, too; I was deeply thankful that he had not to suffer more pain, and that it was I who was called upon to bear the loss of a partner and not him—that in a sense I was allowed to carry the burden of grief and loneliness for him. I was able to receive the comfort that was poured out for me by family and friends, and to feel the love that surrounded me.

Then, after some days, I was hurled from this cherished state of certainty of God's love sustaining me into complete desolation, and I had to realise in my whole being the separation of two people who had been one flesh. I sat numb and desperate in what seemed the wreckage of my life, and the comfort of others could not reach me any more. I only wanted the person I had lost—to see him, to hear his voice, to hold his hand. Grief one could expect to feel, but my own emotions horrified me; above all my anger and resentment at life for dealing me such a blow, and at God, who no longer seemed to care for me. I found myself saying hard and bitter things to those nearest to me and grudging them their easier recovery and enjoyment of life. It was not for some time afterwards that I realised that this anger was for many people of common clay like me a natural accompaniment of acute grief, that it lay deep within me, that other people had felt these emotions before me, and that they would assuredly pass. Other people have told me of their feelings of remorse and guilt, their failure and inadequacy towards the one they have lost. However violent these emotions may be, we have to live through them, perhaps at first just to endure, for the law of life is survival and growth. Yet even in our seeming hopelessness, our feeling that we no longer want to go on living without the one we have lost, we must begin to take the first steps forward from grief and towards life.

The first step is to let go. I found that in my grief I tried to cling to my husband as he had been in life with me, and I had to learn to relax my tight grip, and as one Friend wrote to me helpfully, 'Let him live on and grow and come back spiritually'—perhaps in the same way the disciples had to let Jesus go from them to receive the Comforter, the Holy Spirit, in their lives. The disciples did not receive the Holy Spirit until some weeks after Jesus's death and resurrection, during which time he was able to carry them through a transition period between his earthly presence with them and his presence in the spirit only. Not only had I to let my husband go, but I had also, slowly, to let myself go too, from my first fierce tension of endurance and courage and control into a relaxed trust in God's care and love, and an easy sharing with my family of happy, fulfilled past times that could be relived in the present. This was no quick process with me, and it was another Friend who taught me how to relax in body and mind, and so be liberated from the persisting thought below the level of consciousness that I did not want to go on living without my husband.

Slowly, and even spasmodically, release came in many ways—through the music for which I longed, through flowers and trees and hills, through poetry, through absorbing work, through service to others, through the standing-by of family and friends, through dreams. There were days when I could not feel God in my life any more, although I knew that God existed, when I was numb and when the spirit of joy and delight seemed as though it would never come into my life again. At such times perhaps a rose beside my bed when I awoke would say to me that the divine reality was still there—'He rests here, and is not gone'. The simplest of concrete symbols would help me.

From the earliest days of loss I had longed for what I called to myself 'a word of life' to be spoken to me by someone in my own Meeting. Much affection and help came to me, but not this 'word' I had longed for. Later, in a message given to another in as dire need as my own, it came when a Friend spoke in the meeting for worship of the mystery of personal suffering. He said that we must realise that we are not the only sufferers; we must let our hearts go out to others in our plight, and that will give us perspective. We must thank God for the sensitiveness that let us enjoy to the full the beauty and warmth of the one we have lost, and thank God for the affection and companionship we have had—even give thanks for our sensitiveness

91

in feeling the loss, for we are not mere clods. We must say, 'Though he slay me, yet will I trust in him'. This Friend spoke of the challenge to us to let the agony and trial become creative in moulding us nearer to the pattern of God's purpose for our fulfilment. Lastly, there must be an act of supreme trust—'Yea, though I walk through the valley of the shadow of death, I will fear no evil, for thou art with me'. This message helped me profoundly; it was a rope to which I clung.

Much real help came to me from the understanding of my children and friends, from the simplest expressions of affection that bore the stamp of truth of feeling and 'costingness' (avoiding a second-hand and easy comfort) to the warm welcome into the homes of married friends both young and old—a special help at that time, hurting as it did and healing at the same time. Finally, something that one cannot give to everyone, but that one or two can and do give so tenderly and generously: that is the staying-with another person in the extremity of sadness, just sharing whatever depths there are to be shared with whatever pain may be involved. Not advising, planning, urging, doing anything active (although later all this may have its place) but listening and being there inside the other person's grief and feeling the cost of this. I shall never, I hope, forget this standing-by of another human being in the moment of 'My God, my God, why hast thou forsaken me?' By complete involvement in suffering humanity Christ gave himself in human life. In the willingness to be involved in the pain of another person we can give ourselves in a love that wins the suffering spirit back to life, and helps it to accept its own inevitable residue of loneliness that must be accepted when all that can be done to overcome has been rightly done.

From the first days of bereavement one knows that, as a friend said to me, courage at such times is a top priority. At first the courage to endure, to hold on to the knowledge that God is there whether one can feel that it is so or not. But to overcome grief—to live again—one must grow and move forward. In a practical, physical sense I saw this clearly from the first, and I was greatly helped by being able to plunge into absorbing, worthwhile work. This won me away from the self-pity that is always lurking in the background ready to set upon the bereaved person, especially if he or she must learn to live in a colder climate without family to share with and care for. In my first attempts to make my life worthwhile I threw myself into a full life of service for others: this was good as far as it went, but later I had to learn that one must develop a balance between work, creative interest and warm friendly relationships with others—forming new friendships as well as cherishing old ones. I had to try to stop comparing my present experiences with those of the past to the detriment of the present, to go forward in faith and so, patiently and slowly, find a meaning and purpose and an inward companionship in my new life—a companionship that held within it the one I had lost.

22
Courage to Live By

Courage is not only a priority at times of great personal distress and loss, but an essential ingredient of all life, for as Edwin Muir said, 'This is a difficult country and our home'.[54]

The child going to school for the first time, the young couple starting out for an unknown country and a new job, the mother at the sink and the cooker, the parents parting from their children, the active person facing a breakdown in health or a serious physical handicap, the adults confronting the problems of old age of parents or older relatives, the many with responsible jobs—all need courage, whether of the day-to-day variety or that of the sudden crisis. For myself, I know that I find the actual crisis easier to face, but the hard foot-slogging endurance and faithfulness that must often follow crises I find very hard indeed to attain. The routine patches of life, where we just have to keep on being 'steadfast and unmoveable' find me sadly lacking—yet this sturdiness and robust attitude are perhaps more needed in life than the ability to face crises. These situations are so often with us, for even the most joyful life is a continual striving to confront the problems it raises, its outward and its inward conflicts, and to learn to meet them with an accepting courage that has none of the harshness of the courage of despair.

Life is a compound of joy and woe, of beauty and agony: everything in us rushes out to greet the loveliness and happiness, but we are not so eager to encounter the hardship that is part of life too. It was Paul Tillich who said that all human life can be interpreted as a continuous attempt to avoid despair, and Bernard Miles of the Mermaid Theatre who said that we are put on earth to help other people to endure being alive through joy, through healing and through drama. These statements startle one at first as laying too much emphasis on the difficulty of life, but neither denies the glory and beauty of life, and the statements seem to me to be true. I know in my own life that I am aware of the abyss of non-being and the need for a dynamic and continuing effort of my self towards affirmation. 'Yes, yes, God, and always yes' is a prayer that speaks very much to my condition. In my family two of us would say that we have always been aware of what we call the 'downward drag': the others are of a more sanguine temperament, yet even one of those two would admit to needing to pray for patience every single day in a difficult and demanding situation of personal relationships. For myself, I know the necessity of an act of faith and affirmation every single day of my life.

What is it that we, that I fear? What are these negatives that press in upon us in unguarded moments? Want, toil, insecurity, pain, possible destruction? The feeling of not being able to cope with a special situation? Not being able to preserve our own inner being through grief, mental or physical pain, through torture, through a slow process of grinding down? I know these anxieties for others and for myself. When I lose those dearest to me, I fear that grief may destroy my real essential being, my serenity, my joy. In a nuclear war, it is not death that I fear, but *death in life* —inability to preserve my being, and the inability of those I love to preserve their essential being. Serious illness, acute pain, loneliness, cruelty, all threaten this. I visualise this threat of non-being as a dark abyss of meaninglessness that might open to engulf me and others. It is George Fox's 'ocean of darkness and death'.

Courage is the readiness to take upon ourselves the negatives anticipated by fear—to really face this threat, not denying it or covering it up, for if we merely seem to do this instead of actually doing it the negative elements will break loose from the bundle and show themselves in resentments, bitterness or hard judgments of others. Jesus's life was an overcoming of the powers of darkness—never a denial of their existence. 'The light shines in the dark, and the darkness has never quenched it.' His whole life can be seen as a great story of courage, human courage facing odds. But as we look at it, it seems to change from steadfastness, sturdiness, ordinary courage, into serenity of spirit that embraces courage and goes beyond it.

There is a book called *The Lost Footsteps* by a Rumanian, Silviu Craciunas, which tells the story of a man's bravery in escaping from danger under the Communist regime. His torture, when caught, was so severe that often death would have been welcome, but his spirit commanded his body to go on and it did so. After being flogged, he was forced to run round in a continuous circle and, as he ran, he repeated an incantation he had made up. It was based on an old legend about a sculptor who had begged God to transmute his being into another form and had become a tree with golden leaves, then a sun, then a cloud, then a rock. ' "Lord, change me into a rock", I prayed, "Help me to stand up to these frightening storms; make me

96

strong, so that they cannot break me".' Further torture drove him to an extremity of suffering, and another picture formed in his mind. One evening he saw a chain of snowy mountains gleaming in the sun and in the foreground a little Indian temple and a Brahmin seated under a tall tree. He lived in the company of the Brahmin—a companion who persuaded him that life was sacred and must be lived till the last breath. Craciunas goes on to tell us that though some people are destroyed by suffering, others, through the strength given to them, are challenged by it not only to resist evil but to undertake some positive creative act: some lose control over themselves whilst others grow in grace and strength. 'If you have the blind courage to continue to struggle and to endure, you will find a new beginning to your life.' He discovered an inner serenity and a control of mind and body that resembles that of Jesus in the Gospels: he in his measure discovered the secret of creative suffering, a suffering that produces new life.[55]

George Macdonald said of Christ: 'He came not that men might not suffer, but that their suffering might be like his.'[56] We are not called upon to face the torture of Craciunas, but in our day-to-day situations we are called upon to make our small sufferings creative too. We know, for example, how our own small loneliness can lead to self-pity or to a new understanding of the needs of others and a new ability to meet them. All widening of sympathy is joyful, whether it comes through pain or not.

But what of those times of tedious or painful routine that we must learn to live through and that I personally find so hard? It is only too easy for us at times to see our lives as periods of drabness punctuated by moments of joy and beauty, but are we not really meant to learn to let the moments of elation penetrate our daily lives and spread through them?—those moments when we are deeply aware of the pale gold of the sky, the velvet petals of the rose, the bloom on a baby's cheek, the utter blessedness of father and mother and child, the sublimity of Bach's St Matthew Passion, the trueness of our friends? In many of the Gaelic prayers we feel the all-pervading presence of the infinite in the finite: God is in the milking, he is with the plough, he is in the laying of the fire and in the rains that leave their shining pools. He suddenly confronts man in his fellow man on the road. At the kitchen sink or in the crowded city underground, massed among other human beings, we are finite beings living in infinite time. The moments of ecstacy are our guides. 'They give us light and warmth and direction—and then they are absorbed into us and expressed in the manner in which we continue, in every thought, in every action, every second of existence. For this is the essence of life, the quest for the way, the transformation of moments into a way.'[57] The moments of vision are no longer separated from our everyday life, dreamed of, longed for, but are woven into the very fabric of our being.

Much of life's suffering is comprehensible to us as a product of human free will, but there seems no conceivable justification for a wide area of pain, where an apparently meaningless suffering cuts short lives rich in promise. Time and again one meets this in one's experience and this inexplicable happening can only be met fully by accepting our share of the pain of humanity, as Jesus met his share through the cross, ungrudgingly, creatively. Our binding together in the bundle of life hurts as well as delights. The contingent or chance element in our lives presents us with a real problem. I remember thinking it rather childish of an old couple I knew well to keep saying, after the bombing of their home, 'But why did this happen to *us*? We have always tried to live a good life. Why should *we* be the people who had to lose our home?' Since that time I have lost things more precious to me than my house, and in my heart, if not outwardly, I have repeated their cry of protest.

We have to find a courage that will face this fortuitous element brought about by the working of the universe with its countless combinations and permutations in the world around us and in our own small personal lives. I can in darker moments feel exposed to mere contingency, but I know even in these moments that God's love is with me in every situation in which I find myself. God is indeed in the contingent, facing it with us if we are willing, helping us to use even our worst experiences for good. I know my position to be real and strong when, facing this fortuitous element in life for what it is, I hold fast to that power and love to see me through, placing myself alongside, not leaning in a listless and helpless way. 'I believe that God can bring forth good even from the worst happenings. To this end God needs men and women who can use their circumstances in the best possible way. I believe that in all times of trouble God will give us as much power as we need to meet our trouble, but this is not given to us beforehand, so that we shall not rely on ourselves but on God alone.'[58] This is one of my affirmations for daily living and it is in this faith that our anxiety for the future will be overcome.

Loren Eiseley, the palaeontologist, in *The Firmament of Time*, tells us that the future is grim because 'Western scientific achievement . . . has not concerned itself with the creation of better human beings, nor with self-discipline'.[59] Do we err here in not disciplining ourselves—not with the outward discipline of law, but with the inward discipline of love—and in not helping our children to self-discipline? There is an ego-coddling that is not true love, that makes people feel that they are so precious that they must be wrapped up in cotton wool and not exposed to the wind and rain of life. We have to strengthen our children to find their part in the pattern and live it fully and truly; we must want them to be brave and we must have the courage ourselves to help them to be so, instead of allying ourselves with their retreat. Encouragement does not mean telling other people how nice they are and how nice everything they do is. It means giving them courage to go forward in loyalty to the good they know and to the happiness and beauty and truth that they have enjoyed, taking their doubt as an element that must be absorbed into their faith.

'Lord, I believe. Help thou mine unbelief.' I know how badly I need the encouragement of others, that often my light burns low or almost goes out, and that it is blown into flame again by the courage-bringers that I meet. I know that when I suffer discouragement at the hands of others I am meant to look at this and learn from my unhappy experiences how to help rather than hinder, how to be more tender to the feeling of others.

There are brave words to hearten us: 'March on, my soul, with might' and 'Be strong and of good courage: be not afraid, neither be thou dismayed, for the Lord thy God is with thee whithersoever thou goest'. What can we say now at this present moment just where we are? Do we know to whom we belong so that we can help others to belong, because they see that although we are shaken by the winds of change and adversity we do not break, but are upheld by a power and a presence within and about us, so that we endure because of the joy and the hope that are set before us? Can we go forward saying: 'I arise today through a mighty strength'?

23
Learning to Live Together

The legends of St Columba bring him to us as a real, vivid personality, full of power and strength and tenderness, a man of courage and insight who struggled with adverse forces both within and outside his own nature. His mother, who had a vision about her son's vocation, was said to have given him two names, 'Crimthan' meaning a wolf, and 'Colum' meaning a dove. Both these elements were at work in his nature—the brave and adventurous but fierce and even violent characteristics of the wolf combined with the peace and tenderness and gentleness with which the dove has always been associated. The story tells how St Columba had to come to terms with all the elements in his nature and use all to the glory of God: it was only as he learned to do this that he could become the peacemaker and community-builder of the early church in this country.

We too cannot really love our neighbour as ourselves until we have learned to love ourselves rightly—to accept and understand and value our worth as human beings and members of the vast human family. There are people who seem to do this naturally—who have neither an inflated opinion of themselves that leads to conceit and boastfulness, nor an under-estimation of self that may lead to apologetic uncertainty or lurches from self-abnegation to over-importance—and we love and treasure such fine, balanced natures. But most of us, as well we know, are made up of the wolf and the dove battling with one another, or the thick-skinned rhinoceros and the rabbit, or the lion and the gazelle, and we have the task of accepting our limitations and our natures and bringing all into a whole.

I found it strange that when, some years ago, I was facing a crisis in my personal life, a wise doctor friend said to me, 'Stop trying to be too wonderful!' and she was right. The truth of the matter was that I was trying to be more wonderful than I really was, and the gap between my outward calm and apparent courage and my hidden inner fear and dismay appalled me. Something else that she said helped me too: 'Be as kind to yourself as you would be to one of the students whom you are teaching.' It is not always our problem that we love ourselves too much, but that we do not value ourselves rightly. I can well remember how as a schoolgirl, after the loss of a much-loved mother and the consequent disintegration of the happy home life of our early childhood, I disliked my own appearance so much that I chose in my mind a particularly attractive classmate and imagined myself into her seemingly more desirable life. I even hoped for some years that I might wake up one morning quite a different person. It was the love of other people that helped me to begin to accept myself, and perhaps the process took its most decisive step when I married and had children of my own and knew how I loved each one fully for herself. Then I came to understand deep within me the lovingness of the divine for each one of us just as we are, how we are part of the human family that is loved and accepted, and so are helped through love into being what we are each one meant to be. However much I have fallen away from this thought at times, it is a source of strength and comfort to me and saves me from the ultimate dread and dereliction of isolation—that loneliness and abyss of meaninglessness which is hell on earth.

Jung speaks of our need, first and foremost, for self-knowledge—the utmost possible knowledge of our own wholeness, as he puts it. We must know relentlessly how much good we can do, and what wrong we are capable of, and must beware of regarding the one as real and the other as illusion. Both are elements within our nature and both are bound to come to light within us, should we wish to live, as we ought, without self-deception or self-delusion. This is no complex modern problem, though we are more aware of it nowadays than were our ancestors or at least aware in a different way. How simply some of the finest and most real people we have ever known have lived lives of self-knowledge, humbly accepting themselves as they were, with both dark and light strands in their natures, and going forward from there. But there were also others who did not face the issue squarely, and their successors sometimes shrink from the desire for honesty among younger people today. Jesus often spoke of the need to listen, to see, to understand—as Blake put it, 'To see a world in a grain of sand And heaven in a wild flower'—and showed us that this perceptiveness is more important than the keeping of rules in a rigid way. Jesus never denied the necessity of rules, of law, and we know that we must have rules in family and community life as in national and international life. In the good family the rules are few and clear; as our children grow older the rules require re-examination and alteration as they also do in society as it changes. If they are disobeyed there are obvious consequences, but there is ready forgiveness and compassion and reinstatement.

In today's world people have a great need to know that they matter as persons. Whether we grow to understand ourselves truly or not, we are still conscious of mattering to ourselves very much. Our pains, our interests, our difficulties with other human beings are real and acute. We know well from the comments of other people on our trials that others tend to minimise them and to see them as more easily solved than if they were themselves facing the same situations. Hard as it is to feel other people's trials, we are committed to doing just this very thing, whether it means entering into the friction that has arisen with a difficult neighbour, or the weariness of spirit of a young mother tied to the house and children, or the frustration of a boring job. Perhaps the sharing of joys comes more naturally to us—the happiness of the new baby's arrival, the pleasure of someone else's exciting holiday, the fresh opportunity that has come into someone else's life, the fresh delight that we have ourselves. We all meet people who look at things first from their own point of view, thinking 'How is this going to affect me?' and we know in practice that this attitude does not lead to happier fuller human relations.

We all know at once when people really give us their interest. The glazed public eye, kindly but impersonal, can deny that other people really matter just as much as the hostile or indifferent one. However momentary the contact between person and person may be, it must hold within it the seed of the faith that other people *do* matter. The spontaneous smile of the passing stranger in the street can give us a glimpse of this. Humour, too, is a great sweetener and lightener of life, a reliever of tensions and an important element not only in sharing joys but in the facing of difficulties. Above all, we must be *there* for other people. Christians who stand in the world in the name of Christ have nothing to offer unless they offer to be present, really and totally *in the present*. The failure of so many 'professional' Christians, said John Taylor in *'The Primal Vision'*,[60] has been that they are 'not all there'.

Never to use the person for our own ends, never to possess and to dominate, has consequences for relationships at work, in our friendships and in the home. Cecil Day-Lewis describes movingly the giving of freedom by the parents and the forming of self-hood in the child in his poem, 'Walking Away'. It ends by speaking of a parting with his young son on the school playing field:

> . . . Perhaps it is roughly
> Saying what God alone could perfectly show—
> How self-hood begins in a walking away,
> And love is proved in the letting go.[61]

Love breathes best in a free air. This letting go is often a hard and painful lesson for us to learn, for there is a side of us that longs to cling to what it loves and hold it tight as the little koala bear clings to its mother. We think thereby to preserve love, but find that to keep love we have to set it free.

Again and again in life we have it brought home to us that compassion rather than rigour is our need. We are nearest to God and our fellows when we are moved with love and compassion, and nearest too to our own deepest being. We are furthest away when we are shut off by the hardening and contracting things, the self-absorption that hems us in with our despair, our self-pity, resentment and touchiness, envy and self-importance. Perhaps, above all, it is our habit of judging which is a prime cause of separating us one from another. It sets us over against one another instead of side by side with one another where we should be, striving and searching together, 'not as the good, but as the forgiven'. We help one another best by being completely ourselves, 'warts and all', and by working through our obvious faults and limitations towards a wider hope than hope and faith in our little selves.

Columba combined within his nature the wolf and the dove, and recognising his own diversity must have given him more understanding of the diversity of others. Sometimes we seem to feel that it is a choice of 'either/or' in our relationships with others and in our community life, rather than a combining of different qualities and gifts into one whole. Is there a Quaker image that includes with approval serenity, gentleness and calm, but excludes passion, vigour and movement? Do we find a place for both dove and wolf in our own natures, in those of others and in our community life?

In the Baptistry window of Coventry Cathedral the golden light of the central glass comes out clearly against the rich background of greens and blues and purples and reds, just as the colour of individuality comes out against the background of other and differing personalities. All are there to be treasured with joy and delight and to add their meaning to the whole. We can only lose ourselves in the wider whole, as Jesus showed us that we must do if we are to find ourselves, if we are accepted as differing but essential parts of the whole, in the same way as the loved child is an essential part of the whole family. The individual has a need for the strength and guidance that comes from association with others: we must feel that we are accepted as we *are* so that we may become what we can be. We know what encouragement, warmth and 'heart love' (as Rufus Jones called it) can do for us. Let us give it freely to others, too—'building one another up and helping one another'.

24
A Way In

How encouraging I found it when I first came among Friends to hear those words set at the beginning of the Advices: 'Take heed, dear Friends, to the promptings of love and truth in your hearts'[62]—words that can speak so directly to us all, believers and unbelievers alike. The great thing for me was that it started there at the nub of my experience, with something I knew beyond a doubt—those promptings that laid upon me the burden of discovering how to act in this decision that I had to make today, that new piece of work that I must start tomorrow, that personal relationship that went wrong yesterday and that must be set right by me. I was not asked to make some tremendous statement of belief, but to start with my own experience, both in everyday life and in those heightened moments that come to us all at times of deep happiness or of pain and grief, moments of compassion and moments of bliss and blessing.

I want to speak about some of those heightened moments from my own experience because they seem to me to carry within them the seed of that divine element that made me able to go along with Friends in calling the promptings of love and truth 'the leadings of God'. I shall pick them up at random in my life, and I shall only be able to describe them inadequately because these moments of acute awareness can only be pictured by the poets and painters among us.

I had always longed intensely for a child, and after the birth of my first baby there were many times of sheer beatitude as I sat in the garden or the house with the child beside me, filled with thankfulness and joy for the miracle of her birth. One particular moment stands out from the others when my husband, my child and myself were in the sunlight of our leafy garden together and an unforgettable glory crowned our three-in-oneness. One of my daughters wrote to me of this same experience after the birth of her first child: 'I feel so elated. I just feel happy and for the first time in my life I am really looking forward to the future—it's having this beautiful baby and all going so well and being able to enjoy J to the full and not worrying.'

From birth to death: during times of serious illness and crisis we are often aware of being given an extra supply of strength and endurance. Twice when I have nursed those closest to me in fatal illness I have known not only this extra strength, but I have also been conscious of being made a channel for a love and comfort not my own. As I have held the hand of the other who was near to death I have known a confidence flow through me that was given to me to transmit to the other setting out alone on his or her journey.

These heightened moments which speak of love, of trust, of the sense of being upheld, of joy and creativity, may not have the name of God but do have 'that of God' in them. Here are some of the deepest values that make up ultimate reality, not only for us but for those of other religions or none. Since many of those whom I have most loved have been agnostic, it has always been important for me to recognise and hold fast to the spiritual values that we hold in common. For me, all these experiences draw upon an underlying unity, the ground of our being, which is love. This love I believe to be both within and beyond me, in the experience of given-ness of which I have spoken, while my agnostic friends would say that they know only love within as the transforming power of the universe.

After my mother's early death, whilst I was still a child of twelve years old, I broke away from the Church of England in which I had been brought up together with my sisters. With the literal mind of a child I felt that I had been betrayed by the promise of the church service—'where two or three are gathered together in thy name thou wilt grant their requests'. I and others had requested pleadingly and passionately that my mother should live, but she had died and our happy family world which had been dependent on her serene and loving personality had fallen apart. By the time I was at university I was a very questioning and vocal agnostic who refused to turn to the east in chapel prayers and who had to be asked to leave a Christian apologetics group because I would not cease to query the existence of God. My searches led me to other churches and groups, but it was only after the tragic death of my agnostic father, a noble, gifted and disinterested public servant, that I felt an insistent need to discover a purpose in the universe. During my adolescent years I had been painfully aware of the abyss of meaninglessness that lay beneath my father's useful and active life, because of the loss from which he had been unable to be healed and that had caused the bottom to fall out of his life.

It was a year or two after this, when I was working at the University Settlement in Bristol, that I first came across Friends and was impressed with their approach to life and with the freedom and spirituality that seemed to permeate all they did. I asked two of them to take me to a Friends meeting for worship; I wanted to see where these fruits of life came from. I do not remember the messages that were given, but I knew that in that quiet place of listening and waiting I had found the spiritual home I had been longing for, and that in the quietness there was for me as for those others the source of strength and joy, peace and freedom that I call God. I knew God there with me and in those others who sat beside me; I was not the initiator, and all I and they needed to do was to be responsive to what was given, whether in the order of nature, in the world of relationships or in the secret places of my own heart. Later I was to discover that this contact with the divine—the experience of the Inner Light—is the central message of Friends. But there and then I forgot my body, my unusual surroundings, my thoughts and emotions, and was aware of being gathered into a healing peace and of going forth cleansed and refreshed and strengthened.

For a time I was well content to rest in this experience, which I underwent again in the many Friends' meetings that I quietly and persistently visited, though the degree to which I experienced it varied. It was only after I was established in this expectant waiting that I began to read and study and discuss the beliefs and practices of the Society of Friends. I understood from the outset the link between the source of love and strength drawn upon in meeting and the fruits of the spirit that were shown in daily living, for it was a deep and understanding love for others that had first attracted me to find the source from which it came. I had seen it in the work of the Quaker hospital almoner who treated each patient with care and respect, in the study group working for international understanding, in the wise and tender treatment of problem children. The belief that God is in every person, that each is precious and that our response is to show an understanding love for others, however difficult they may be, found a ready response in me.

Before this experience I had often been dissatisfied and distressed with the pieces of life's experience around me, some happy, some terribly sad. They lay about me like so many different disconnected bits of the jigsaw puzzle of existence. I knew that it was essential for real life to make a final leap into synthesis—an act of reflection that would satisfy emotion and reason and that would be an act of faith. No one could do this for me—I would have to do it myself. There is a bird of the Northern European forests called the common golden-eye; she lays her eggs in a hole in a tree and when the young are hatched out, the female flies down and sits calling on the ground below the tree. One after another the downy young scramble to the entrance and throw themselves fearlessly to join their mother twenty or thirty feet below. We can remain on the brink as many fine and sensitive people do, afraid that the final leap may involve us in intellectual dishonesty or in a committal for which we are not ready. But into an integrating faith, whether religious or humanist, it seems that we must leap.

There are those who have grown up through a steady, nourishing faith into an increasing awareness and acceptance that makes no leap necessary. But for many like myself there has been a period of doubt and breaking away from the traditional beliefs and practices, a time of searching and striving and a final battering on the door in emotional or intellectual or spiritual need or a combination of these. I knew that in order to do justice to my experience as a human being, I must find out what life was for, what I was, who I was and to whom I belonged. My desire and my longing were the starting point, my importunity and insistence the battering ram. Jesus, with his spiritual insight, commends the importunate widow, the friend at midnight asking for a loaf of bread—asking, asking and asking again until the door opens. It may seem as though all the strivings are on our part, yet we may come to find, as I did, that we were being searched for before we began our search.

I first came to know God as a source of power and peace and truth in the quietness of meeting for worship and in my own restless heart. But how then did Christ come in and how did I find the companion to whom I listen, to whom I speak, the God Blake speaks of in 'I am not a God afar off, I am your brother and a friend; Within your bosoms I reside, and you reside in me'?[63] We make our guesses at the nature of God, and we are often like my small daughter who said, 'My mind goes round and round when I want to think about God, but I can think of Jesus.' To me Jesus is a window through to God, a person who in terms of personality, in a way that can be grasped by our finite minds, shows what mercy, pity, peace are like in human life. I turn to the Jesus of the New Testament—to his healing word, his freedom from anxiety, his outreaching insight, to him as a whole person—not to imitate him but to let him live and grow in my life.

His message, as given through his teaching about the Kingdom of Heaven, in his parables and in the Sermon on the Mount, expresses eternal truths. His life of love and truth and trust and communion with the divine convinces me and persuades me, so that I understand why early Friends spoke of the 'Inner Light' as synonymous with 'the indwelling Christ' and of themselves as 'humble learners in the school of Christ'.

I do not pray to him—I look at him, dwell upon him, love him. But it is the presence of the God he worshipped of which I am conscious as I look at the night sky, the sleeping child and the rose. When I listen in the quietness and when I pray, it is to God that I listen and pray. And since personality is the highest value that I know in life, since all truth comes to us through the medium of human minds and thoughts, I am not surprised that God too comes to me in terms of personality. I can well understand how to many Christians Christ comes as a tangible figure, a Son of God in a special unique way, even though that is not the way he comes to me. Every word that comes to our lips is a symbol, and the symbol of the father God has been sanctified by Jesus's use of it as well as by how it has been used throughout the Bible. We have much to learn about the image of fatherhood, and from the growing and developing idea of God in the Old Testament. Now we may be beginning to learn about God the mother as well.

I have learned among Friends that our minds must always be open to new light 'from whatever quarter it may come'[64] and we know that our understanding of God must not be static but dynamic. It is only too easy for Christians to worship a God who is too small, and to have too limited an idea of what love and compassion mean in action. We know how humbling and enlightening it is to encounter others who are far ahead of us in this. The clues we are given to the meaning of life are not necessarily labelled 'Christianity' or 'religion' and through narrowing down our experience of what we regard as 'religious' Christians may miss the clues which those who live to the full in their practical tasks, their family life and varied contacts, in community work or politics or the arts and in many other fields, may find. In the life of the spirit we grow by openness to the light we have received, to the new light that is always coming to us and by obedience to this light in our lives; the blinkers of too narrow a field of experience may shut us off from the richness of life.

'I came that you might have life and have it more abundantly', said Jesus, and his words have been echoed down the years by many who have given their lives in disinterested love for others. Life is meant to be rich, full, all-embracing, and a religion that misses out whole areas of experience because they are secular is not the total response of the person to the whole environment that a true religion should be. We can observe this in some rigid sects, but we need to watch it in our Society with its multiplicity of committee meetings and business meetings making their claims upon our time.

How are we to be helped in our search and our response, and to the change that our response inevitably brings to us? Very soon we come up against the plain fact that we ourselves are not adequate for the task; if we attempt it in our strength alone we shall find it a heavy burden of responsibility that we cannot carry. But, as we commit ourselves to following the way of trust and love and reconciliation and forgiveness, we find that we are not left alone in it. We are no longer working against the grain of the wood of life, but with it. We are no longer straining over the many pieces of the puzzle that seem to have no connection with each other, but realise instead that all will even-

116

tually fit into the whole to make a picture—that there is a whole. We realise that one has gone before us on the way and that as we commit ourselves to making God's insight and healing word our own, we shall learn in our own experience who God is. It is no outside authority that persuades me of the truth of Jesus's words: his presence has reality in my life because his words convince me in my mind and heart.

A wise old Friend, when there was much discussion among a group of younger people as to what they could or could not accept as truth in the New Testament, said, 'Take the gospels and underline everything in them that persuades you of its own truth. Leave the rest and start with that. You will be surprised how much there is that convinces you of its truth and relevance to life as we are living it today.' We have to be prepared not only to observe that truth, but to respond to it and be willing for the change that it brings about in us; we need, too, to support this change in others. For the change that disturbs our complacency and our pride will be compensated for by the sense of freedom, peace and satisfaction that it gives us.

The divine companion comes under many guises and is revealed in many images, but knows what we are and asks for the whole of us. The sense of presence is given to us and we are asked to be present in our turn. It is in resting in this awareness of presence that we are given the power to commit ourselves. Early Friends well knew this need in personal and corporate life to know God in the silence, to listen and to be responsive. We push on in our busy, talkative, active lives and wonder at the power, serenity and clearness of those early Friends. We try to explain it by the difference between our distracting modern age and the more leisurely times in which they lived, but there is no doubt that they held to the vital importance of making a pause in life, of remembering, attending, listening, responding. George Fox's voice insists quietly but firmly, 'Be still and cool in thy own mind and spirit from thy own thoughts, and then thou wilt feel the principle of God to turn thy mind to the Lord, from whom cometh life; whereby thou mayest receive his strength and power to allay all storms and tempests. That is it which works up into patience, innocency, soberness, into stillness, staidness, quietness up to God, with his power.'[65] The more recent voice of the Advices continues, 'Yield yourselves and all your outward concerns to God's guidance . . . Seek to know an inward retirement even amid the activities of daily life. Make a quiet place wherein you may learn more of the meaning of prayer . . . Bring the whole of your daily life under the ordering of the spirit of Christ.'[66]

There are many who think that religion is now a personal and private matter, that public worship is outmoded. But Friends' experience of meeting together 'in the presence of God and one another' is that with diversity but the same spirit, our individual relationship with God becomes part of a group experience, and that our sense of union with God is bound up with our unity with one another. In waiting together in silence and expectancy, in being 'tendered' as early Friends called it—made aware and open and tender-hearted to the needs of others—in sharing

118

the divine communication, we are preserved from relying on the fallibility of our individual guidance. The group can be a strength and a check, and in the group meeting for worship we may know our individual experience extended and enriched. 'It is not the scattered embers, but the piled up logs that send leaping flames to heaven.'

There is no substitute for the stillness in which the presence becomes known—in solitude, together, in flashes, in scattered clues, through our imperfect vision in part only—known as taking the initiative and confronting us on the road. We start with the inward promptings of love and truth in our hearts, those leadings of the beyond in our midst; we travel from that which is within to that which is beyond. In our varying ways and at different times we know the divine as father or mother, companion, sister or brother; as healing strengthening light or cherishing love. God becomes real to us through many images, and it need not trouble you too much that your images are not mine, so long as we share the revelation that our God is walking the road ahead of us. 'The world is charged with the grandeur of God.'[67]

References

1. *Collected Poems and Plays of Rabindranath Tagore*. London: Macmillan, 1936, poem xv, p. 182.

2. *Advices and Queries*. London Yearly Meeting, 1964.

3. Walter de la Mare, 'Go far, come near' in *The Inward Companion*. London: Faber & Faber, 1956.

4. Georg Wilhelm Hegel, *Lectures on the Philosophy of Religion*. Trns. from German by Speirs & Sanderson. London: Routledge, 1962.

5. *Advices and Queries*, op. cit., III.

6. *Matthew*, 6:28 (RSV).

7. Clive Sansom, 'The Flower of Time' in *The Friend*, vol. 117, 7 August 1959.

8. Gerald Bullett, 'In the Garden at Night' in *Poems*. London: Cambridge University Press, p. 40.

9. Last line of a song from the play 'The Women-Hater' (Act III, Scene 1) in *The Dramatic Works in the Beaumont and Fletcher Canon*. Ed. F. Bowers. London: Cambridge University Press, 1966.

10. Rabindranath Tagore as quoted in *From Darkness to Light* by Victor Gollancz. London: Gollancz, 1964, p. 107.

11. George H. Gorman, *The Amazing Fact of Quaker Worship*. London: Quaker Home Service, 1973.

12. *Ibid.*, p. 131.

13. George Fox, *Journal*, ed. J. L. Nickalls. London Yearly Meeting, 1952, p. 19. Entry for 1647.

14. William Penn, *Some Fruits of Solitude* quoted in *Christian Faith and Practice in the Experience of the Society of Friends*. London Yearly Meeting, 1960, §190.

15. George Fox, *op. cit.*, p. 19.

16. Rainer Maria Rilke in *Later Poems* trans. by J. B. Leishmann. London: Hogarth Press, 1959.

17. Neville Ward, *The Use of Praying*. London: Epworth Press, 1968, p. 21.

18. Barbara Hepworth, untraced.

19. Rilke, *op. cit.*

[20] *Advices and Queries,* op. cit., III.

[21] George Fox, quoted in *Christian Faith and Practice* op. cit., §376.

[22] *Philippians,* 2:15.

[23] George Fox, *op. cit.,* p. 19.

[24] John Keats in a letter to his brothers G. and T. Keats dated 21 December 1817 in *The Life and Letters of John Keats.* London: Dent (Everyman's Library), 1927, p. 62.

[25] *Advices and Queries,* op. cit., III.

[26] Dietrich Bonhoeffer, *Letters and Papers from Prison.* London: SCM Press, 1971.

[27] Dag Hammarskjöld, *Markings* trans. W. H. Auden. London: Faber, 1966, p. 144.

[28] Howard Brinton, *Quaker Journals: varieties of religious experience among Friends.* Wallingford, Pa. USA: Pendle Hill Publications, 1972.

[29] George H. Gorman, *op. cit.,* p. 85.

[30] Winifred Rushforth, *Something is Happening.* Gateway Books, 1981, p. 59.

[31] Frederich von Hügel, *Selected writings* compiled and introduced by P. Franklin Chambers. London: Collins (Fontana), 1964.

[32] Walter de la Mare, 'Winged Chariot' in *A Choice of de la Mare's Verse.* London: Faber, p. 217.

[33] *Advices and Queries,* op. cit., Query 13.

[34] *A Letter of James,* 3 and 4.

[35] Henry T. Hodgkin (1877–1933) untraced.

[36] Richard Church, 'These words' in *Richard Church* (Pocket Poets). London: Edward Hulton, 1959, p. 29.

[37] Dag Hammarskjöld, *op. cit.,* p. 110.

[38] Dietrich Bonhoeffer, 'A wedding Sermon from a Prison Cell, May 1943' in *Letters and Papers from Prison* ed. by Eberhard Bethge. London: SCM Press, 1953.

[39] William Blake, 'Everlasting Gospel' in *The Penguin Poets: William Blake* ed. J. Bronowski. Harmondsworth, Middx: Penguin Books, 1958.

[40] Dag Hammarskjöld, *op. cit.,* p. 165.

[41] George Eliot, *Middlemarch.* Various editions.

[42] T. S. Eliot, 'East Coker' in *Four Quartets.* London: Faber, 1944, p. 22.

121

[43] *Advices and Queries*, op. cit.

[44] *Ibid.*, III.

[45] Lily Pincus, *The Challenge of a Long Life*. London: Faber, 1981, p. 17.

[46] Books by Peter B. Townsend, *The Development of home and welfare services for old people, 1946–60*. Assn. of Directors of Welfare Services, 1961; *Family life of old people: an enquiry in East London*. Routledge & Kegan Paul, 1957; *The Last Refuge: a survey of residential institutions and homes for the aged.* Routledge & Kegan Paul, 1962; *Personal, family and social circumstances of old people*. Intern. Assn. of Gerontology, 1959.

[47] Eric Holttum, 'God and humanity' review of 1982 Swarthmore Lecture *Reasonable Uncertainty* by Gerald Priestland in *The Friend* 1 October 1982, p. 1229.

[48] Anne Ridler, 'Nothing is lost' in *Poems of Today*. London: Macmillan, 1963, Fifth Series, p. 108.

[49] Kitty Grave, *A Pool of Quiet: meditations for a month*. Friends Fellowship of Healing, 1981.

[50] Ladislaus Boros, *The Moment of Truth*. Tunbridge Wells: Burns & Oates, 1965.

[51] Konrad Braun, 'Rediscovering the Bible' in *The Friend* 2 September 1966.

[52] Arnold Toynbee, *Experiences*. London: Oxford University Press, 1969.

[53] Walt Whitman, 'Song of myself' in *Leaves of Grass*. London: Harrap, 1949, p. 31.

[54] Edwin Muir, 'The Difficult Country' in *Selected Poems*. London: Faber, 1965, p. 82.

[55] Silviu Craciunas, *The Lost Footsteps*. London: Collins & Harvill, 1961.

[56] George Macdonald, untraced.

[57] R. Dorac, 'Moments of Ecstacy' in *Hibbert Journal.*

[58] Dietrich Bonhoeffer, *Ethics*. London: SCM Press, 1971.

[59] Loren Eiseley, *The Firmament of Time*. London: Gollancz, 1961.

[60] John V. Taylor, *The Primal Vision*. London: SCM Press, 1963, p. 197.

[61] Cecil Day-Lewis, 'Walking Away' in *Poems of C. Day Lewis 1925–72*. London: Cape and Hogarth Press, 1977, p. 234.

[62] *Advices and Queries*, op. cit., I.

[63] William Blake, 'Jerusalem' in *William Blake's Writings* ed. by G. E. Bentley. Oxford: Clarendon Press, 1978, Vol. 1 'Engraved and Etched writings', p. 421.

[64] *Advices and Queries*, op. cit., III.

[65] George Fox, *Journal* ed. J. L. Nickalls. London Yearly Meeting, 1952, p. 346. Quoted in *Christian Faith and Practice*, op. cit., §303.

[66] *Advices and Queries*, op. cit., I.

[67] Gerard Manley Hopkins, 'God's Grandeur' in *Major Poems of Gerard Manley Hopkins*. Dent: Everyman, 1979.